Blood Money
The Method and Madness of Assassins

"This is a work of nonfiction. No names have been changed, no characters invented, no events fabricated."

by: RJ PARKER

ISBN-13: 978-1987902341
ISBN-10: 1987902343
Copyright and Published (2017)

by RJ Parker Publishing
www.RJPARKERPUBLISHING.COM

Published in United States of America

Copyrights

This book is licensed for your personal enjoyment only. All rights reserved. No part of this publication can be reproduced or transmitted in any form or by any means without prior written authorization from <u>RJ Parker Publishing</u>. The unauthorized reproduction or distribution of a copyrighted work is illegal. Criminal copyright infringement, including infringement without monetary gain, is investigated by the FBI and is punishable by fines and federal imprisonment.

Book Links

AUDIOBOOKS at RJ Parker Publishing
http://rjparkerpublishing.com/audiobooks.html

Our collection of **CRIMES CANADA** books on Amazon.
http://www.crimescanada.com/

TRUE CRIME Books by RJ Parker Publishing on Amazon.
http://rjpp.ca/ASTORE-TRUECRIME

ACTION / FICTION Books by Bernard DeLeo on Amazon.
http://bit.ly/ACTION-FICTION

RJ Parker Publishing

Follow on *BOOKBUB*

"This is a work of nonfiction. No names have been changed, no characters invented, no events fabricated."

Blood Money: The Method and Madness of Assassins

Table of Contents

Book Links..5
Foreword..8
Introduction...13
The Dark Web..15
A Brief History..19
Mechanics of Contract Killing................................24
Organized Crime and Contract Killers....................29
How do Contract Killers Operate?..........................33
Types of Organized Crimes.....................................37
Statistics of Contract Killings.................................42
Known Employers of Assassins..............................47
Jorge Ayala – Cocaine Cowboy's Hitman...............59
Are Contract Killers Still Operating?......................64
Myths of Modern Day Contract Killing..................68
Vincent Coll – Mad Dog..73
Marinko Magda – The Serbian Shooter..................82
Christopher Dale Flannery- Mister Rent-a-Kill........87
Cold Blooded Professional Killers..........................94
Charles Harrelson – Natural Born Killer.................98
Richard Kuklinski – The Iceman...........................105
Alexander Solonik – Agent 47...............................114
Giuseppe Greco – The Goodfella..........................126
Glennon Engleman – The Dentist..........................135
Benjamin Siegel – Bugsy.......................................145
Female Assassins that Took the World by Storm....154
Contract Killers in Fiction.....................................159
Joseph Sullivan – The Mad Dog............................163
Chester Wheeler Campbell -The 007 of Detroit.....172
Wayne Perry – Silk..181

Harry Strauss – Pittsburgh Phil..............................188
Conclusion..195
About the Author..197
    Contact Information...199
    The Basement...200
    Serial Killers Encyclopedia...............................201
    Parents Who Killed Their Children....................202
Appreciation...203
References..204

Foreword

Contract Killers vs. Serial Killers

by Dr. Scott Bonn

There is some debate among criminologists, psychologists and law enforcement authorities as to whether professional assassins or so-called hit men should be considered serial killers. Moreover, there has been considerable debate among experts for decades over the exact criteria and definition of serial murder itself.

During the past forty years, multiple definitions of serial murder have been used by law enforcement officials, clinicians, academicians and researchers. While these definitions normally share common elements, they differ on specific requirements such as the number of murders required, the types of motivation and the temporal aspects of the murders.

Although it was modified by the FBI in 2005, the classic definition of a serial killer is one who has taken the life of at least three victims in separate crimes, scenes and events, and where there is an emotional cooling-off period that separates the murders.

In contrast to serial killers, "hit men" are professional contract killers employed by organized crime groups to eliminate their rivals or other troublesome individuals.

One of the most infamous of all professional hit men was Vincent "Mad Dog" Coll who, despite the fact that he was Irish, committed dozens of contract murders for the Italian Mafia in New York City in the 1920s. He gained infamy for the accidental killing of a young child during a mob kidnapping attempt. Coll's exploits have been chronicled in numerous books and Hollywood films such as *Mobsters* in 1991.

Unlike serial killers who select their own victims, the targets of hit men are carefully chosen for them by their employers who pay them to kill on demand. Although professional hit men and serial killers share the common characteristics of killing multiple victims in separate and unrelated events, hit men are not serial killers because their motivation to kill is strictly financial. The murders committed by professional hit men fulfill no emotional or psychological needs on their part. Serial killers such as Ted Bundy, on the other hand, are driven to murder by fantasy and powerful emotional needs such as lust or excitement.

A unique exception to the clear distinction between serial killers and contract killers is the late Richard Kuklinski who was both a serial killer and a professional hit man. When he wasn't committing contract killings for the Gambino crime family, Kuklinski was killing strangers who irritated or annoyed him. He claimed to derive great pleasure and exhilaration from the challenge of killing his victims. Kuklinski was given the nickname "Iceman" for his method of freezing a victim to confuse the time of death.

There is another important distinction that separates serial killers from professional hit men. Serial killers experience an emotional cooling-off period between their murders during which time they blend back into their seemingly normal lives. In contrast, professional hit men do not experience/require a cooling-off period between their murders because of the unemotional and pragmatic nature of their killings.

During the cooling-off period between murders, a serial killer disappears from the public eye and resumes his/her seemingly normal routine and life. Incredibly, the life of a serial killer during the cooling-off period, particularly if he/she is a psychopathic killer like Ted Bundy—that is, pathologically devoid of emotion or empathy—may appear completely normal to the unsuspecting observer.

Serial predators reemerge from a cooling-off period to strike again when the urge to kill becomes overwhelming to them. A serial killer may not even understand his/her compulsion to kill but knows that it is both undeniable and uncontrollable when the urge arises.

The cooling-off period between murders is

highly subjective, unpredictable, and it varies from one serial killer to another in terms of its duration. The length of the cooling-off period can also vary between murders committed by the same serial killer. The duration can be from days or weeks to months and, in rare instances, even years.

For example, notorious serial killer Dennis Rader or "Bind, Torture, Kill" (BTK) confessed to ten murders that he committed over a span of nearly twenty years (1974-1991) after he was captured in 2005. In between his murders, Rader lived a remarkably normal-looking outward life with a wife and two children. He was perceived as a pillar of his community in Wichita, Kansas.

Inwardly, Rader was secretly satisfying his sexual needs and delaying his compulsion to kill for months and even years at a time through autoerotic fantasies in which he relived his murders with the aid of trophies taken from his victims such as articles of clothing, identification cards and jewelry.

As a result of this practice, the length of the cooling-off period between Rader's murders was highly variable and often lasted much longer than other serial killers. His ability to control his compulsive need to kill for years at a time through autoerotic fantasy is highly unusual for serial killers.

Unlike serial killers, professional hit men do not experience such inner compulsions to kill. Their motivations lie outside themselves and are financially motivated.

Blood Money: The Method and Madness of Assassins

I applaud my friend, RJ Parker, for undertaking this project, and for examining an important category of multiple killers that are often depicted, and even romanticized, in book and film but is rarely properly explained.

Scott Bonn, PhD

Criminologist and author of the bestselling book *Why We Love Serial Killers: The Curious Appeal of the World's Most Savage Murderers*.

(06.06.17)

Introduction

The contract killer has consumed the mind of the average person for quite a length of time. There seems to be an air of mystery when it comes to contract killing that is truly unmistakable, one that comes from their shadowy nature due to the fact that their identities are difficult to ascertain while they are still active. Contract killers have very short careers and life expectancies which is why they tend to be so intriguing. The short careers add a bit of romanticism to their overall aura, something that definitely boosts public interest and makes them far more likely to be heavily researched.

Before one delves into the sordid details of contract killers, their history and what makes them who they are, one first needs to understand what a contract killer is. Essentially, a contract killer is someone that is recruited to kill somebody for a fee. They are hired by a wide variety of people, from organized crime syndicates to individuals that just bear a grudge against others. Their targets include heads of rival organized crime syndicates, politicians, successful businessmen and even regular people that ended up crossing the wrong person or have someone who is out to get them.

All in all, contract killers are a part of society that we might rather ignore, but at the end of the day, it is very important to realize that they represent facets of our society that we must analyze in order to understand where such violence comes from. In the following pages, you are going to learn about some of the most famous contract killers in history, what brought them to that point in their lives, as well as the various iconic depictions of hit men in the film and television industry and how this reflects on how the public perceives contract killers.

The Dark Web

There are several Hitmen for Hire sites on the Dark Web. Some, like the Chechen Mob, charge between $5,000 and $200,000 for murder, depending on the target and the difficulty of the job.

The Chechen Mob site is a dangerous marketplace that can be accessed with the Tor Browser at http://5nr3yoxhbgzprocb.onion . This is a special onion address accessible only in Tor Browser; it won't work with other browsers. I STRONGLY SUGGEST YOU DON'T ACCESS THIS ADDRESS OR EVEN ENTER THE DARK WEB. I DID WHILE RESEARCHING FOR THIS BOOK AND IT WASN'T LONG BEFORE I HEARD FROM THE FEDS.

Blood Money: The Method and Madness of Assassins

It says:

"This Website is under investigation and its data has been seized by the National Crime Agency (NCA) and the Bulgarian National Unit for Combatting Serious Organized Crime.

If you have visited this website for the purpose of using its services or have previously used its services you could have committed a criminal offence, including solicitation to murder. In the UK solicitation to murder can carry a penalty of life imprisonment.

The NCA and international law enforcement partners are identifying and prosecuting the users of this website. The NCA will continue to pursue the users of services such as these on the dark or open web."

The Chechen Mob site, for example, is basically an eBay for illegal services, allowing gang members worldwide to sign up and provide services. Customers can also sign up and purchase services.

This is for informational purposes only. I do not encourage anyone to hire their services.

Customers and gang members hide their IP addresses while accessing such sites. They also transact payments in Bitcoin, a digital currency that is hard to track.

After Silk Road made millions of dollars in 2013 by providing drug dealers with a way to sell their drugs online, many mafia organizations released sites on Deep or Dark Web to offer various services, including drugs, guns, counterfeit currency, and fake IDs, as well as body harm services.

These sites are difficult to close by FBI and law enforcement because their IP is hidden and their hosting is offshore. Many sites stay low and fly under the radar, relying on word of mouth to get new customers, without allowing search engines to index them.

A part of their members, gang members from all over the world sign up to provide services, getting 80% of the price paid by customers, while the Chechen Mob gets 20%.

Blood Money: The Method and Madness of Assassins

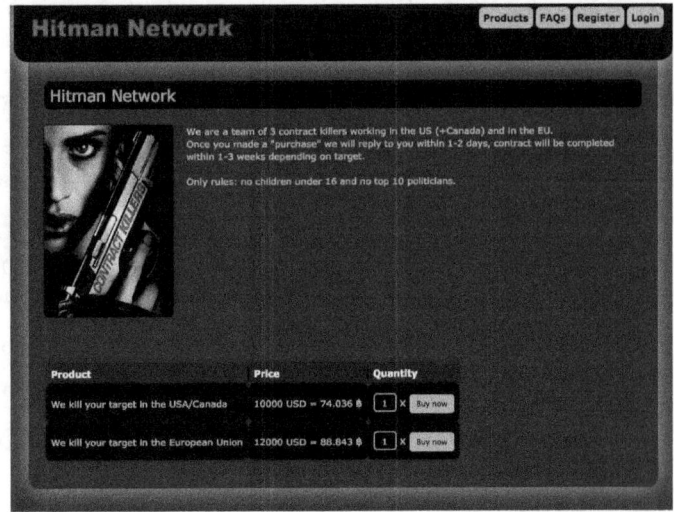

I found this site on the Dark Web. It's currently being investigated by the FBI and Interpol. On their site it says that Hitman Network does draw a line between what it will and will not do: "*no children under 16 and no top 10 politicians.*"

A Brief History

People have been hiring assassins since the dawn of civilization. There was a distinction made between the two main groups of fighters that would kill for money. One group was called mercenaries while the other group was referred to as assassins. Mercenaries were essentially soldiers that powerful people could hire if they did not have men that would fight for them out of loyalty. They were also often used to supplement existing armies and make them stronger, thereby ensuring victory in battle. Assassins were a different breed entirely. They were never hired in bulk; rather the hiring of an assassin was a far more secretive affair. Assassins were used for stealth missions; they were used to kill individuals. Powerful people in these olden days used assassins to kill army generals and rival kings and thus acquire additional power for the person that did the hiring in the first place.

While the origin of the word "assassins" comes from a group of armed men that killed for money based in the city of Masyaf in modern day Syria in the 11th century, the act of assassination itself is ancient. While there are is no evidence that could prove that assassinations occurred before recorded history, there are mentions of people getting assassinated in sources such as the Old Testament.

The Old Testament was compiled in the year 400 BC, but the individual scriptures that were eventually combined into the Old Testament are far older, and describe events that occurred centuries prior at the very least. This means that assassination, by extension, killing people for money, was a part of public consciousness well before the modern usage of the term contract killer was invented. Although it evolved to be slightly different in modern day times, the origins of the contract killer can be traced back to these assassinations, thus proving that this profession is actually quite old and probably will continue to have a part to play in our history for a long time yet to come.

Contract killing was not restricted to any particular geographic area. While mass media has created the image of a contract killer and made this image out to be stereotypically western, killers for hire have been prevalent in pretty much every country in the world. One example of contract killers in parts of the world that you might not have expected is in China. In the eighth century, which was during the Tang dynasty in China, there was a high-ranking official named Li Fuguo who was a personal advisor to the Emperor of China. After the Emperor's death, he quickly became the sole figure in the imperial court and was set to become more powerful than the new Emperor himself until he was assassinated by contract killers that were sent by the person he was supposed to serve. The new Emperor, son of the one that Li Fuguo had gained his power serving, was afraid that Fuguo would supersede his own importance and that people would start obeying him.

This was how dynasties fell at this point in China's history, so the Emperor's sentiments were understandable.

What you might have noticed while tracing this ancient history of assassinations and contract killings is that the vast majority of the time, they were used by people who had some kind of political motive. Caesar was assassinated by people who thought that he had too much power in one of the earliest examples of assassination being dramatically depicted for entertainment as Shakespeare showed in his iconic work "Julius Caesar". Things have not changed all that much in modern contract killings either. The only difference is that contract killing is usually not state sanctioned. Instead, the rival kingdoms consist of crime families, and their political machinations are based on the control of illicit substances and the profit that can be derived from such substances.

Throughout the Middle Ages, contract killing was rife in the Byzantine Empire, with the services of these assassins mostly being acquired in order to kill a king or emperor. During this period in time, contract killers were a very popular way to take control, and this resulted in several centuries of anarchy which plagued empires all across Europe.

This became far less common during the last few centuries of the previous millennium. Apart from the fact that most kings and emperors during this time had their security optimized in order to ensure that they did not get killed; contract killing had become extremely predictable as well. However, this did not diminish its continued use as a tool for power. Some of the most prominent assassinations in the modern era were of Presidents of the United States of America, with one of the most famous examples being the assassination of Abraham Lincoln only days after his victory in the Civil War. Apart from the four successful attempts, there have been a great many unsuccessful attempts on the life of the American President as well, since this individual tends to be extremely powerful and killing him would serve the interests of a great many people. Even so, most of these assassinations were not conducted for money; the people who committed these acts were not paid or contracted by an individual with competing interests. Instead, these assassinations were conducted generally for personal reasons, although it can be argued that John F. Kennedy's assassin might have been paid.

There have been instances where contract killers were used by heads of state rather extensively in spite of the fact that, in the modern era, this had started to become a great deal less common. For example, Joseph Stalin had a lot of people assassinated for his own political gains. He essentially did this to strike fear into the hearts of the people he was ruling over, thereby ensuring that they would not think about revolting. These contract killers were sanctioned by the state which made them a part of the government, one of the most recent examples of something like this occurring.

Overall, contract killing has remained in the area of organized crime. The origins of modern organized crime with the influx of immigrants in the early part of the 20th century ensured that contract killing survived into the modern era, but it was extremely popular for criminals in the Old West as well, with contract killers serving an important role before western states such as North Dakota and the like were annexed by the government of America.

In the modern era, there are a number of examples of celebrities and such getting in on this type of thing as well, including NFL players and musicians, all of whom have hired or tried to hire a contract killer to murder someone in their lives. It is important to note how prevalent this type of activity has remained. While it was originally used for political motives and is now generally used in organized crime syndicates with some very rare usage for politics serving as outliers, the general approach has remained the same. A killer is hired, given a contract, and that contract is used to ensure that the killer does what he is supposed to do.

Mechanics of Contract Killing

The process of hiring a contract killer is a rather complex one. Most organized crime syndicates have one that they hire on a regular basis, one whose services they consistently use in order to ensure that they always have someone on hand if they need someone killed. If these contract killers are not hired on a permanent basis by these criminal organizations, they are generally acquired through various channels. Such organizations have contacts in places where contract killers are usually found, and they can use these contacts to hire freelancers, as it were, individuals that work on a job-by-job basis.

There is one peculiarity of contract killing that is very important to note. This peculiarity has to do with the very name of the act. Contract killing seems to imply that there is actually some kind of contract that has been signed. The truth of the matter is that there is usually no contract at all. Instead, contract killers are assigned targets and they are supposed to hit these targets as quickly as possible, thereby making it easier for the crime organization they have been hired by to go about their business.

That is because the task that they are being paid to perform is illegal in and of itself. This makes any contract that might be signed inadmissible in a court of law. The whole purpose of a contract is ensuring that both parties honor their agreements. This includes the party that has been hired to complete the task that they are going to be paid for, as well as the party that did the hiring in the first place. In a contract, the amount that would be paid is decided and set in stone. The purpose of doing this is to ensure that both parties stay true to their word. In the vast majority of cases where people end up creating a contract, they want to prevent any mishaps from occurring while the contract is in effect.

If the client does not pay up after the task has been completed, if the hired party does not complete the task but asks for money, or if there is some disagreement on the amount of remuneration that is to be received, the contract can be used in a court of law to settle the matter. The problem here is that this only applied to contracts pertaining to legal activities.

Since there is no legal contract, technically there is nothing forcing the contract killer to do the job. In addition, the person that hired the contract killer has no legal obligation to pay the individual after they have completed the task that they were assigned, and any arguments over the amount that is going to be paid would obviously have to be settled outside of court. And yet, in spite of all of these factors, contract killings still occur on an extremely regular basis, and they are a part of how business is conducted in the underworld.

The question that needs to be asked is how exactly do contract killings occur if there is no overarching structure that would enable the people involved to get some kind of assurance that they are going to get paid? What you must understand is that a complex code has developed that enables contract killers and the people that hire them to work with one another. In essence, people that are ranked highly in the criminal underworld tend to care a great deal about their reputation. Hence, they are not going to renege on their contract since this would make them look bad and would make them lose the respect of the people that are working for them. Contract killers also have the same kind of dynamic. They are going to remain consistent in their work and will always try to provide the best result possible because this would help spread the word regarding their endeavors which would help them get even more work in the future. When a criminal is surrounded by other criminals, reputation is going to matter a great deal; otherwise, you would not know who to trust. Hence, both mob bosses and contract killers alike would be eager to provide frequent assurances that they are never going to renege on their contract in any way.

Nevertheless, at the end of the day, these people are dealing with criminals on a daily basis. There is really only so much that one can do when trust is all that you are depending on. Hence, threats of violence are also often made. It is generally going to be a lot more difficult for a contract killer to get their payment if a mob boss refuses since this leader of an organized crime syndicate would have a number of different people that would be able to strong arm the contract killer into accepting the consequences of what has happened.

This is why contract killers generally only work for people that have contacts. Additionally, contract killers try their best to obtain as much information as possible, thereby ensuring that no matter what happens, they would have the arsenal they need in order to ensure payment. In many situations, contract killers tend to take advance payments so that they know that the person hiring them has the money to afford them. In most cases, contract killers working for organized crime syndicates are going to get an amount of money that would be used for their day-to-day expenses and the like. This is to ensure that they do not run out of money and run into problems while they are on the job.

One thing that keeps both parties in check when it comes to contract killing is the fact that they are both generally afraid of each other. One of the parties is a man that runs a criminal organization that would pay to have others killed, while the other is the sort of person that kills others for money and does so in cold blood. Neither of these parties can be considered particularly savory, so this certainly would have an impact on the success and prevalence of contract killing in general.

All in all, the manner in which contract killings are conducted is rather mysterious, which adds greatly to the mystique of the practice. All that is truly known is that contract killers generally seem to get their money, although one thing that should be noted is that they are not paid as much as people seem to think. Low-level contract killers have been hired for rates as low as a few hundred dollars, and some of the more high-end contract killers are known for working at rates that go for a few thousand dollars. This is paltry compared to what people usually think, which is that contract killers earn tens of thousands of dollars for a single kill and live lavish lifestyles. In truth, they are probably no more visible than regular people, and in fact are probably more anxious than most people would be to fit in so that their draconian occupation does not end up coming to light.

While contract killing in this modern era is still a mysterious practice that not a lot of people know the details about, the manner in which it was conducted during the past few decades and centuries has been recorded, and it can provide some necessary insights into how contract killers do their business. In the next chapter you are going to read about contract killers over the years and how they used their skills to influence the course of history as well as how they featured in people's normal everyday lives when they killed lower level targets.

Organized Crime and Contract Killers

One reason that contract killers tend to be so prevalent in the world of organized crime is that they provide mob bosses with the opportunity to commit acts of war against their rivals without actually starting an all-out conflict. Contract killers are specially trained to attack people that have a lot of personal security; rival mob bosses are constantly under threat of being hit. Still, they are not the only people that organized crime targets. Apart from targets that are within the circle of organized crime, one example of a prime target for a contract killer is a politician.

Politicians play a bigger role in organized crime than you may think. Even though criminals are breaking the law, for the most part they need to follow certain rules and regulations simply because they would not have a choice. For example, when they are trying to get a shipment of drugs into the city so that they can sell them for profit, they are going to need a politician or a corrupt cop to make the process smoother.

This is where contract killers come in. Bribery is often a very effective way of making sure that politicians and corrupt police work for the mob, but often more drastic measures need to be taken. These measures involve threatening these individuals with a hit. Money is a very good motivator, but at the end of the day, it's not the sort of thing that can make anyone do anything. There are going to be people that have principles, people that would not want to take part in organized crime because they feel like it would be the wrong thing to do. If an organized crime syndicate absolutely needs these individuals to cooperate, a really good way is to threaten to have them killed. This makes it a choice between their principles and their lives, and the vast majority of people are going to choose the latter.

Additionally, people that the mob has bribed might end up asking for too much. They would think that they have dirt on the mob that they can use as blackmail. Such people can be highly dangerous for any organized crime syndicate and will have to be eliminated. What better way to ensure that this happens than hiring a contract killer? After all, this is exactly what they are trained to do.

Apart from politicians, one of the most common targets for contract killers are witnesses. These witnesses are often in way over their heads. They have no idea the danger they are in and so think that they can go to the police and tell them what they know about the mob. Often, a member of a criminal organization may start to snitch after he gets arrested in order to reduce the jail time he is facing.

These people can be taken out by contract killers, thus insulating the mob in question from any snitching done by former members that are now in the hands of the law. If the snitch in question is not accessible, possibly because he is in a highly secured location in order to ensure his safety until he testifies, contract killers are often hired to go after their families in order to make them keep their mouth shut. The general process here is that one family member would be injured or killed, and the snitch would know that if he talks, the rest of his family is going to die as well. This is a highly efficient way of ensuring that people don't end up testifying against the gang that they were once a part of.

Of course, one of the mainstays of pretty much any contract killer's career is going after people that are not paying up. There are a lot of different people that come into this category. The mob might have given drugs to someone on the promise that he would pay later, but now he is trying to weasel his way out of a payment. Someone might have robbed a mob stash house, something that can be seen as an enormous sign of disrespect. In such situations, the contract killers are often instructed to make their targets highly visible after they are killed so that nobody thinks of doing anything like that ever again.

Small-time contract killers are used in this manner as well. Essentially, they are used to bully people into paying for protection. If people do not pay up, a contract killer would be hired to take them out so that everyone else in the neighborhood knows what is going to end up happening if they don't do the smart thing by paying up.

Contract killers also often branch out into

other areas as well. Organized crime is a vast world where the possibilities are endless. Contract killers are famous for branching out into areas such as drug trafficking, gun running and the like. For their services to their crime family, they are given the reward of higher status, and with this status comes the prospect of taking part in some far more profitable enterprises than just contract killing.

Overall, organized crime is one of the biggest reasons why contract killers are so famous in this modern day and age. While it is true that the majority of contract killers are not involved with the world of organized crime, the ones that are certainly end up becoming far more notorious than the ones that aren't. This has contributed enormously to the public image of contract killers and has resulted in a lot of them using this publicity to get profitable book and film deals. It is safe to say that if it had not been for organized crime syndicates across the world, contract killers would be pretty much unheard of at this point, although this is something that a lot of contract killers would have preferred since it would have made them less likely to come in the line of fire.

How do Contract Killers Operate?

The manner in which contract killers operate can differ greatly from one killer to another. This is because they tend to be extremely varied in their approach, with each killer bringing his own unique personality to the fore. The reason that contract killers are so difficult to catch is that their modus operandi often results in them taking care of any evidence that might lead to their capture. One of the biggest examples of how contract killers often create problems for police officials is the fact that they change up their techniques as well.

Generally, the modern myth that contract killers operate using high-tech equipment from the shadows could not be more false. In truth, contract killers are known for their ability to adapt to the situation at hand. They don't have the time to set up heavy equipment as snipers do, and one of the biggest reasons that they are so widely renowned and in demand is because they don't need such gadgets either.

There is also the simple fact that the vast majority of contract killers simply can't afford high-end gadgets like this. Such things can end up costing enormous amounts of money that the average contract killer simply does not have access to. As a result, the praise that contract killers generate is a product of necessity as well as preference.

General Modus Operandi

The basic manner in which contract killers function is that they accept a contract and study their target before doing anything else. This is the most important part of their process because, without it, they would be completely unable to kill their targets without leaving a huge trail of evidence.

The length of this reconnaissance depends on how much money the contract killer is getting paid, how much time he has to complete his job and how difficult a target he has been assigned. People tend to think that contract killers spend weeks before making a kill, but more often it's just days and sometimes even hours.

Understand that the amount of time contract killers spend on their kills is so short is because the longer they delay, the less likely they are going to be able to complete the contract. Their target might notice that they are being spied on, and in many cases, contract killers end up losing their nerve. You can't really blame them – they are human beings, too, after all!

Once the reconnaissance and intelligence-gathering process is complete, the contract killer will attempt to intercept the person he is supposed to kill while they are going about their normal routine. Contract killers are unlikely to break into someone's home because this would raise a great deal of suspicion and would make it quite difficult for them to get out of there without getting caught – breaking and entering could alert their targets to the fact that something was about to happen. They might end up calling the police which could cause enormous problems for the contract killer. Additionally, breaking into the target's house might get the killer seen by one of the neighbors. Said neighbors might end up telling the police that they saw someone, and if their description is accurate, that would be the end of the contract killer's career since he was definitely going to get caught based on the testimony

Catching the target while they are going about their normal routine allows contract killers to use the element of surprise. Their target would be caught unawares, and if the contract killer acted quickly enough, they would be able to make the kill and walk away before anyone even knew what had happened. This seems like a rather dangerous way to go about things, but it works surprisingly well which is probably why so many contract killers have adopted this practice.

The weapon of choice tends to matter a lot. Guns with silencers are a very practical option, but the problem here is that they often cost quite a bit of money, which is why so many contract killers prefer to use more creative methods for reducing noise caused by gunfire. One common technique is to cover the gun in a thick t-shirt. While this would certainly not work as well as a proper silencer, it would certainly provide the contract killer with some kind of sound-muffling effect, and this can go a very long way.

Tradition Trumps All

One very important thing to note about the way that contract killers operate is the fact that they have been using a lot of the same techniques for many years. The guns may have gotten a bit more powerful and sophisticated, but at the end of the day, the only thing that really matters is making sure that the target is taken down, and since there are already so many techniques that have been tried and tested, most contract killers choose not to experiment too much.

There have been cases where contract killers used poison instead of traditional techniques. Poison is a very useful tool for a contract killer because it can allow them to kill their target without being seen at all. Instead of having to worry about leaving the scene of the crime once their target is dead, they would be quite far off to begin with and would thus not have to worry about clean-up at all. One thing to keep in mind about this particular technique is that it results in a lot of problems when forensics comes into play. If the contract killer used a rarer poison, it could end up getting traced back to them. Interestingly, women tend to use poison more than men. This might be because they lack the physical strength to take down larger men, but a lot of other reasons could come into play as well that have nothing to do with strength.

Types of Organized Crimes

Organized crime comprises a wide range of activities, all of which are essential to the functioning of the criminal underground. The important thing to note is that all of these activities function within the same ecosystem, so the success of one activity can lead directly to the success of another. Here are the various types of organized criminal activities:

Protection Rackets

These are the bread and butter of the traditional gangster. Protection rackets are well known for providing stable income for mobsters, and they are widely popular because of how simple they are to start and how easy they are to enforce.

A protection racket essentially involves someone with a lot of muscle extorting small business owners. A mob boss would do so by entering a place of business, breaking a few things and threatening to keep coming back if the business owner does not agree to pay for "protection". Some mob bosses would take the promise of protection seriously, shielding paying business owners from corrupt police officers and more brutal gangs. Other mob bosses, on the other hand, would essentially just be threatening people for money, and would often inflict violence upon people even after they had paid for protection.

Drug Trafficking

If protection rackets are the mainstay of low-level crime, drug trafficking is where the bigger fish go to earn their money. This is possibly the single most profitable criminal venture in the world because it provides mob bosses with a consistent, stable source of enormous income. Drugs are incredibly addictive, so criminals would take advantage of this by giving samples out to people, getting them hooked, and then capitalizing on their addiction.

The reason that drugs are so profitable is that buyers will do pretty much anything to get the money to buy more. Hence, consistent sales were not a problem. The only real problem was the police. Since drugs are such a menace to society, mob bosses dealing in drugs need to be a lot more careful about how they go about their business. Often, corrupt police officers have to be bribed as do low-level judges. All of this is done in order to ensure that the mob bosses do not end up facing any heat for the fact that they are involved in drugs.

The criminal underground deals in a large variety of drugs. Heroin is the most profitable since it is the most addictive, but it brings with it enormous police interest. Cocaine is highly valuable because it is used by the upper-class crowd and thus can command quite a hefty price. Marijuana is a low-level drug that does not offer that much monetary gain, but it has served as a good starting point for criminals that want to enter the drug game with a lower than usual investment and without inciting nearly as much ire from the police department.

Prostitution

Prostitution has always been a tricky game because police monitor it a lot, but mob bosses that have established themselves thoroughly in other areas of crime often enter this world because they want to take their profits to the next level. Prostitution comes in all shapes and sizes, and depending on the importance of the person employing the prostitutes, their rates can be either dirt cheap or unbelievably expensive.

Often, the most high-end prostitutes are called escorts and have nothing to do with organized crime. Gangs and crime families tend to go for brothels and bordellos instead, offering low to mid rates for customers that appreciate secrecy.

One aspect of the prostitution game that is notable is the fact that it incites a great deal less violence. Turf wars are almost nonexistent when it comes to prostitution, and the market is not contested as heavily as it is when it comes to drugs. Hence, a lot of mob bosses opt for prostitution in order to avoid violence since nothing can bring the police down on you as hard as gunshots will. Prostitution rings are often closely tied with drug rings, but it is not uncommon to see mob families specializing in them as well.

Gambling

There are a lot of states where gambling is still illegal, and in these states, it is organized crime that provides avid gamblers with a space in which they can indulge themselves. This criminal activity is more of a throwback to a more puritan time in American history. Not that long ago, gambling was illegal throughout the country. Crime families had both the organizational skills as well as the manpower to set up a gambling ring and enforce payments, two things that were absolutely essential to potential gamblers feeling safe enough to put up their money.

Arms Dealing

The sale of high-grade weapons has often proven to be an immensely profitable enterprise because of the high value that these guns demand. While Italian and Russian crime families tend to avoid this business, black gangs, the Irish mob and the Yakuza all excel in this field and provide weapons to the majority of other criminal elements within these areas. Thus, an interesting point to note is that in the purchase of firearms and the like, even opposing and rival crime families would have a sort of respect for one another. This code is a big part of why organized crime thrived in the first place.

Bootlegging

During the prohibition era, criminal organizations made huge profits by trading in liquor. Since alcohol has always been and will always be in high demand, people were willing to pay a premium in order to gain access to it, even though it was now an illegal substance. When the prohibition era ended, many criminal organizations failed to find other sources of income and ended up falling apart within a few years. This is partly what led to them turning to drugs as a new source of profit.

Statistics of Contract Killings

The statistics of contract killing vary widely from place to place. Generally, around 2 to 5 percent of all murders that occur within a given year will have been committed for money. This is true across the globe, with the vast majority of contract killers following this trend, regardless of their nationality.

One example can be found in Australia. Although the murder rate in Australia is far lower than in the United States, the proportions remain the same. A university in Australia conducted a study that proved this. Two hundred murders were selected at random, all of them having been committed over the past seven years. It was found that four percent of these had been committed by a professional who had been paid for the job.

If you look at America, approximately thirteen thousand murders were committed in the entire country last year. Roughly four hundred of these were done on a contract killing basis. If you pull out a calculator and do the math, you will notice that the percentage rate has once again remained consistent.

This poses a rather interesting question. How is the rate of contract killing so similar throughout the world? One of the best answers to this question lies in the prevalence of organized crime itself. Organized crime is an entity that cannot be controlled, an entity that regulates itself and will not be removed completely no matter how much the police try to make that happen. Organized crime comprises the same fraction of every country's economy because in this modern day and age of globalization, police practices are roughly similar throughout the western world and have comparable rates of success. Hence, since the proportion of organized crime is going to remain similar throughout the world, the rate of contract killing is going to remain similar as well because contract killing is inexorably linked to organized crime. They have a symbiotic relationship because one cannot function without the other. Crime bosses are always going to need contract killers in order to consolidate power, insulate themselves from legal threats and ensure a steady income from their various criminal interests. Similarly, contract killers depend on organized crime in order to earn their living. Killing is their bread and butter, and there is no entity that needs the services of a contract killer more than an organized crime syndicate.

Assuming that the prevalence of contract killing is owed entirely to the various organized crime syndicates in the world would be simplifying things enormously. Things are never that simple. The fact of the matter is that while organized crime may be the source for most of the stories surrounding contract killers, the truth is that the vast majority of contract killers are not involved with organized crime in any way, although they probably wished they were since gigs like that tend to pay enormous amounts of money and result in long-term security and growth opportunities within the context of the criminal underworld.

No, the vast majority of contract killers kill for people that are just regular folk who have a grudge against somebody. One of the most common contracts that these killers fulfill is a revenge contract. This is usually offered by someone that is angry at their spouse or significant other for having been unfaithful to them. In their rage, they hire somebody to kill their spouse or partner as revenge for their infidelity.

Even more common than the revenge kill is the insurance kill. Lots of people have life insurance these days, and lots of people have financial problems as well. This combination results in many people hiring contract killers to have other people killed. A lot of times the target is the client themselves. They want to be able to provide for their family, and they know that their life insurance benefits would give them the money they need to live a long and happy life that is full of comfort.

Most of the insurance kills that contract killers are paid for are not nearly as noble, though. More often, someone would hire a contract killer to kill a relative or someone else that they act as an heir to or are a beneficiary of in an attempt to cash in and retire in comfort.

Since the most common instances of contract killing have nothing to do with organized crime, it is safe to say that the prevalence of contract killing is intrinsically intertwined with the human psyche.

Humans are, by their very nature, vengeful folk. They don't like being slighted; they don't like being embarrassed. In addition to this, a lot of people out there are very desperate for some kind of solution to their endless financial problems. Contract killers offer these people the chance to satisfy their thirst for vengeance or get a solution to their financial problems.

Hence, if you really think about it, the main reason why contract killers are so prevalent is because there are always people that are willing to hire them. Since, once again, we live in a globalized community, the feelings and emotions that people share are more or less standardized, which means that no matter what country you are in, most people are going to react the same way to similar situations.

The statistics of contract killing result in some fairly interesting figures, but at the same time, they offer unique insight into the way the human mind works. They are a reflection on human civilization as a whole. This is not surprising; contract killers are a highly underrated source of psychological data. These people usually go for serial killers and the circumstances that create them, but contract killers are much subtler beasts. Perhaps one of the reasons that they are not studied as much as serial killers is because serial killers are outliers – people have nothing in common with them. Contract killers, on the other hand, tend to hit uncomfortably close to home. They show us a side to ourselves that we usually try to keep hidden, and this more than anything else is why people are more afraid of them than they would care to admit.

Known Employers of Assassins

Assassins are not the only people at fault when you think about it. Also at fault are the people that hire them in the first place, people that are known for their other crimes and use their enormous power and influence to cause much misery unto others.

There are a few mob bosses throughout history that are well known for hiring contract killers. These criminal masterminds are in many ways the people that ended up creating the modern contract killer, molding him and turning him into what he is. Their need for killing is what brought about the birth of contract killing in the first place.

Listed below are some of the most notorious gangsters that hired contract killers, all of whom played an intrinsic role in making contract killing what it is today. From Russian Mafia to Italian Mafia, Irish Mob to Jewish, each and every one of these criminals has helped to provide professional killers with extremely stable sources of income which they used to further their influence in the world of crime and eventually attain enormous respect for themselves, going on to create large criminal empires of their own as well.

Dutch Schultz

Dutch Schultz is very much an example of what organized crime was like during its earliest days. The prohibition era was what truly gave rise to organized crime because it provided these mob bosses with something they could sell at a premium but was not that difficult to procure. Schultz was involved in a wide range of illicit activities, but one of the activities he was most known for was bootlegging because he was so successful in it.

Additionally, he was widely involved in the illegal gambling rings that had set up around this time. Once gambling was outlawed in the vast majority of the country, Schultz saw that he finally had the opportunity to rise above his competition completely and take part in something that could make him the big bucks. One of the most important features of his gambling rings was the fact that they were so safe. In spite of the fact that he was a criminal, Schultz put a lot of effort into ensuring that his illegal gambling dens were extremely peaceful places. Violence was absolutely not tolerated in these places.

One reason why this was the case had to do with the fact that the police were often willing to turn a blind eye towards criminal activities that did not involve that much violence. If a criminal organization was taking part in some business, the only thing that would make the police want to take an interest would be if the criminal activities were causing some kind of violence because this was something that they were going to end up being answerable for. Hence, Schultz put a lot of effort into avoiding violence so that the police would never find out where his gambling lairs were.

Another big reason why he was so eager to avoid violence in his den had to do with the fact that it made the environment a little more welcoming for his customers. He was offering a service that thousands would want to take part in, so the only thing that could possibly cause a problem here was the fact that people often shied away from places where organized crime activities were occurring. They would feel unsafe in these areas, which meant that Schultz could potentially lose a lot of money if no one ended up coming to his gambling dens. He handled this problem rather well by offering a safe environment. Whoever came to Schultz's gambling hideaway knew that, no matter what happened, he would not have to worry about getting hurt. Since there was no violence, police would take no interest in these gambling places either, which meant that the patrons of these illicit but thriving establishments could gamble in peace knowing that there was no way they would get caught.

One of the most important facts about Schultz's career is the fact that he was one of the first people to offer a kill contract. He was responsible for the hiring of Vincent Coll, one of the very first contract killers in the history of the profession in its modern context. He would pay Coll to kill people for him, offering him money on a per-kill basis. This set a template that the vast majority of organized crime syndicates would end up following in the future.

This was how Schultz ended up giving birth to modern contract killing. Even though he and Coll eventually had a falling out, the fact that he had started this practice makes him an extraordinarily influential figure in the history of killing people for money.

Charles "Lucky" Luciano

Schultz was extremely successful during his time, but his position as the king of organized crime on the east coast was taken by a far more adept criminal. The man that took the throne away from Schultz was known as Charles Luciano. People called him Lucky because of his skill at poker as well as his tendency to always come out on the other side without a scratch. What people did not know was that it was his skill rather than his luck that allowed him to always escape bad situations completely free from harm and legal liability.

He was just as old school as Schultz was, and so he was involved in many of the same rackets as his rival. The only difference between them was that Luciano was a far more adept manager and strategist. He used his talents to ensure that his criminal syndicate always remained free from any legal liability, and in a unique move, he ended up getting Schultz arrested by providing the police with evidence of his crimes.

Luciano was more than just a mob boss. Even though he was a respectable boss in his own right, his true power lay in his abilities as a kingmaker. Luciano was the only Mafioso during this time who was on good terms with pretty much every single family, even those families that had rivalries with his own. He used his talents to create a criminal empire that was the first of its kind.

Before Luciano, the criminal element in America was comprised of a bunch of bickering gangs that fought over tiny strips of territory and were barely able to earn any money before the police ended up taking them down. Luciano knew that if organized crime was going to survive and succeed, he was going to have to make sure that these fights ended for good. This was why he organized a council on which the head of every single mob family would sit. Territory would be apportioned based on merit and influence, and the gangs and families that did not get a lot of territory were compensated in one way or the other. What this did was that it made it easier for mobs to work alongside one another. Violence from one criminal to another began to drop drastically.

Yet, there is another side to Luciano's establishment of the criminal council. One of his closest colleagues was a man by the name of Benjamin Siegel. Siegel is widely considered to be one of the most successful contract killers in history. Siegel was one of the first people to take part in contract killing, much like Vincent Coll. Even so, much in the same manner that Luciano ended up enjoying a lot more success than his contemporary Schultz, Siegel enjoyed far more success than Coll ever did. His career lasted a lot longer and his influence ended up becoming so widespread that he established his very own contract killing syndicate by the name of Murder, Incorporated.

Hence, Luciano was responsible for the proliferation of contract killing in America. While he was certainly not the first person to hire such people (Dutch Schultz did it first), it can be argued that Luciano did it a lot better. He organized it, monetized it and turned it into a legitimate business. It is safe to say that without Luciano, contract killing would never have become as widespread as it is today. He successfully used Siegel's talents and set a template that would be followed by mob bosses hiring contract killers for decades to come.

Al Capone

Al Capone was almost a contemporary of Luciano and Schultz, but his fame and rise to power came a little later than theirs did. After Luciano had established his criminal operation and had apportioned territory to the various criminal entities that existed throughout America, Chicago started to become a much more profitable criminal locale. This is because it became an extremely important part of the drug trafficking trade, providing a pit stop between the east and the west states.

Capone was the first person to completely unite Chicago. His use of force was legendary, as was his keenness to use contract killers. He was known for having a continuously rotating cycle of contract killers that he would hire time and time again for a period and then would cut them off entirely. He did this so that he would have limited liabilities.

Thus, Capone began to turn Chicago into New York's rival when it came to crime. He was able to use his mental faculties to prevent his arrest for many years, and during these years, he donated a lot of money to charity. Baseball stadiums, schools, hospitals, all kinds of public places received money from Al Capone. This made him famous as a philanthropist, with many going so far as to call him a modern-day Robin Hood.

Capone was so involved in charity because he knew that this was the best way to insulate himself from the long arms of the law. Since his public image was so bright and he was so well loved within his community, Capone became untouchable for the police. The very mention of his arrest would cause public uproar, and this meant that the police were never really able to get close to him. Another reason that he was safe from the police had to do with the fact that he was far too clever to leave any evidence behind. He was involved in a number of criminal activities, but he always made sure that no evidence was left at the scenes of his crimes and that there was always a fall guy that would go to prison for him in exchange for his family being taken care of so that Al Capone would stay safe.

Police were truly stumped about how they were going to arrest Capone, and it was not until the Federal authorities came into the fray that there was any real chance of arresting him. Capone was widely known for his donations, but the question that no one seemed to ask was, where did these donations come from?

Capone had set up a number of shell companies that he used to launder his money, and the vast majority of these companies were instrumental to making his earnings seem legitimate. However, it is important to take into account the fact that his charitable donations often exceeded what he would have been able to afford even when taking into account his fabulous wealth.

The FBI took advantage of this and started looking into his finances. They proved that he was spending more than he was earning, which meant that he had undisclosed sources of income. Although these illegal sources of income were never found as Capone was too smart, the presence of this income in and of itself was enough to have Capone sentenced to prison. He failed to live through his relatively short sentence of eleven years because of heart problems. In the seven years he ruled over Chicago, Capone brought the idea of contract killing to the city and showed people what contract killers could really do.

Pablo Escobar

There is a misconception out there that contract killers are solely hired by members of the Italian mafia. This is not true at all. Pablo Escobar was one of the most powerful drug lords in history, earning hundreds of billions of dollars over the course of his extraordinary life. He was also well known for his use of contract killers, and the unique way in which he used contract killers was that he would hire them to kill people in different countries for him.

Escobar grew up in Medellin in Colombia. He became involved in crime at a very young age and quickly made a name for himself as a master strategist as well as an extremely capable manager. Using his talents, he began to expand into things like the selling of black market goods. It was not long before he became involved in drugs.

While he initially found a great deal of success in the selling of marijuana, Escobar had always had bigger plans for his career. He eventually found someone that had fled Peru after a revolution and had left the drug trade there in tatters. He had a technique for making very pure cocaine. Before this point, cocaine had been a rather difficult drug to obtain, and it was largely unpopular because it was so impure and dangerous. Nevertheless, the cocaine that Escobar now had access to was a different beast entirely. It was the sort of drug that would get people uncontrollably addicted, and he saw the enormous potential in that.

While he did have the chance to make reasonable profits by selling the drug in Colombia, Escobar knew that if he truly wanted to earn the money that he deserved, he would have to think a little bigger. Escobar knew that in America, people were willing to pay exorbitant prices for drugs. All they wanted was a way to get high, and they had the money to pay whatever it took to get that high. Escobar decided to take advantage of this.

Blood Money: The Method and Madness of Assassins

He started shipping his cocaine out to America where he sold it for enormous profit. He had so much money that he spent thousands every day on rubber bands that he used to tie the money up. Escobar saw success that few, if any, had ever seen before or since, and this was why it became so important for him to hire contract killers.

You see, he had a lot of enemies in America. Gangs were annoyed that the Colombian cartel was starting to make so much money in areas where they had ruled for so long. Escobar had the prospect of perpetual war on his hands, and he knew that this could end up ruining his entire operation. He had a lot to handle in Medellin and so could not go all the way to America in order to lead his men in this war. Hence, instead of taking part in these wars himself, he hired contract killers to take out the people that were causing trouble for him across the border.

These contract killers were enormously adept at getting the job done. Escobar's use of contract killers was one of the first instances of contract killers being hired from across the border to do a job in the Western hemisphere. Although Europe had been doing things like this for some time now, the Americas had never seen anything like it; thus Escobar was able to take his enemies by surprise. Contract killers allowed Escobar to maintain his hold over America and earn obscenely large amounts of money in the process.

Frank Costello

While Luciano definitely deserves his title as the father of modern organized crime, he could not have done it alone. He had the help of someone by the name of Frank Costello. Costello started his crime career at an earlier age than Luciano, but by the time he met his future partner, he had already made quite an impact on the world of crime and had started to make a name for himself.

When Luciano started to talk about organizing the crime families into a single council, Costello was one of the few people that supported him from the very beginning. His logic was that he believed in Luciano's work ethic, and thus was on board with whatever Luciano would use him for.

When Luciano was arrested, it was Costello that ended up saving his crime family from falling to pieces. He assumed the role of leader and became a strong and decisive one, and one of the most important things that he did was that he incorporated the profession of contract killing even further into the dynamic of criminal organizations.

Murder, Incorporated, was starting to break apart, and Costello saw this as an opportunity to capitalize. He began hiring a lot of the contract killers as hired guns and gave them a steady income. He was also frequently on the lookout for new people to join the gang and provided a lot of young contract killers with their first paychecks.

The thing that makes Costello such a seminal figure in the world of contract killing is that he allowed it to continue. Luciano was the controlling force, Costello was the driving force. Luciano had put in place an incredible system that allowed contract killers to thrive, but if it had not been for Costello, this system would have collapsed after Luciano went to prison and eventually settled outside the country as part of his plea bargain.

Not everyone involved in organized crime had an enormous role to play like Luciano and Costello did, which is why these two are so well thought of and why they are still considered legends these days to criminal enterprises that see the enormous benefits that these individuals have provided. Whether you look at it from the point of view of organized crime or contract killing specifically, Luciano and Costello were the people without whom this profession would have died out only a few years after it had been invented.

Jorge Ayala – Cocaine Cowboy's Hitman

While the Italians and Irish dominated the East Coast, the South American cartels were making a name for themselves in Florida where the drug business was really starting to boom. One drug in particular was starting to get insanely popular, a drug by the name of cocaine. Miami, Florida, was a hard-partying city, and everyone in this city loved a drug that would allow them to party even harder. The Colombian cartel finally had the inroad they needed to make vast amounts of money, but in order to ensure that this money supply would remain consistent and would not be put at risk, they needed contract killers working for them within Miami.

Jorge Ayala was one such contract killer. He was part of a gang called the Cocaine Cowboys who handled a lot of the criminal activities in Miami on behalf of the cartel. Over the course of his career, he became widely known and respected for his ability to kill with theatricality, thus showing all of the enemies of the cartel who they were supposed to bow down to.

Early Criminal Career

Not much is known about Ayala's early life. All that is known is that he entered the States during his late teens as an enforcer for the cartel, and he slowly worked his way up until he became known for contract killing. As an enforcer, he was not initially given the standard payment per-kill contract that most American contract killers were offered, but after expanding and making contacts in the underworld, he realized that he was missing out on quite a bit of money. This was when he decided to work as a contract killer and branch outside of the Cocaine Cowboys.

Initially, though, Ayala's criminal career revolved around his gang. He worshipped the gang's leader and did exactly what he was told, something that would contrast starkly with the later stages of his career. He made a name for himself through his willingness to inflict extreme violence upon the people he was assigned to kill; as a result, whenever there was a particularly nasty target that needed to be taken out, Ayala was the one that was inevitably called.

He used a variety of different techniques during his kills. One of his favored kill techniques was to behead his victim. Unlike many of the cartel enforcers that had started this practice in an attempt to assert their dominance over a particular territory, Ayala did not kill his victims before chopping their heads off. Rather, he would use the process of beheading as the kill method in and of itself.

Increasing Recognition

His violence allowed his cartel to gain control over Miami, and once drugs started to flood into the city, Ayala became very rich indeed. Due to his faithfulness to the cartel, Ayala was given control of large portions of the drug trade in the city. This meant that he now had men to do his killing for them. The problem here was that Ayala hated not being able to kill. He had relished the prospect of killing when he had been an enforcer, and he missed it sorely now. The rush of killing was the only thing that made him feel alive.

This was when he started using his contacts to find kill contracts that he could complete. The problem was that Ayala was known for grandiose kills, and often his new job required him to kill a little more discreetly. This was entirely at odds with Ayala's own personality, but he managed to pull his kills off by adapting to the needs of his clients.

His career as a contract killer created tension among his fellow gang members. They started to claim that he was no longer as faithful as he had once been to the cartel, that in carrying out tasks for potential rivals, he was betraying his gang family. Ayala responded to these accusations the only way he knew how: by killing the people that were making them.

Thus, Ayala solidified his hold over his corner of Miami, and he reigned as its bloody king for nearly a decade before his inevitable downfall.

Capture

The thing about Ayala was that he was not the sort of criminal who would last very long. He was too bold, too much of a risk taker, too arrogant. Eventually, the string of murders that he had committed caught up to him. He became a wanted man when police found evidence that he had committed several murders. This prompted Ayala to flee the state, and he managed to avoid capture for several months.

Finally, in 1986, Ayala was arrested in a bloody shootout where he killed several members of the State Police. His trial was swift, and Ayala was sentenced to life in prison. He came into prison an absolute legend. This meant that he was able to acquire a small fraction of his former power within those four walls.

In spite of his frequent attempts to get his sentence reduced due to good behavior, Ayala ended up dying in prison. The Cocaine Cowboys had ended up breaking apart not long after Ayala's arrest, but the legacy he and his fellow cartel members had left behind would end up influencing Miami, and Florida as a whole, for decades to come. Even now, Florida remains one of the most popular entry points for cocaine in the country, and many of the contacts that Ayala had once used to smuggle his drugs in are still active, although they are far less violent than they were before.

Are Contract Killers Still Operating?

Contract killers are still very much prevalent in our modern society. Organized crime has gone nowhere, police have won some minor and a few major battles but the war most certainly rages on. There are a lot of crime families out there that are taking part in the criminal underworld and need the services of a contract killer on a regular basis. This is one of the biggest reasons why contract killers still exist, although there are certain differences in how they tend to operate.

Shift to the Internet

One of the biggest differences between the contract killers discussed here and the ones that are operating currently is their prevalence on the internet. Before, trying to find a contract killer was a messy and often dangerous business. It resulted in a lot of people getting killed because they were not looking in the right places.

The internet has made a lot of things very different and, in many ways, has made the acquiring of goods and services highly convenient and efficient. As such, contract killers have taken advantage of this dynamic and have begun to advertise their services online.

As mentioned at the beginning of the book, while it is true that they do not advertise openly at all and you are not going to find any trace of them in the part of the internet that you generally surf, there is a section of the world wide web where contract killers as well as numerous other criminals are highly prevalent. This section of the internet is called the "Dark Web". It is part of a larger part of the internet called the Deep Web. The Deep Web essentially refers to sites that cannot be accessed through normal means. You can't discover them through normal search engines, and so few people stumble upon them by accident. Instead, if you want to go to the Deep Web, you will need to know exactly where to look.

The Dark Web refers to a section in this Deep Web that takes advantage of the lack of visibility to conduct illegal activities. From the sale of drugs and firearms to the airing of snuff shows, this part of the internet is notorious for being a hub for the most depraved members of society. It is in this part of the web that you would be able to find contract killers.

One of the major differences between how contracts were originally made is that you often never even meet the killer you have hired. Rather, you just send the details of the person you want killed to your online hire and then sit back and wait for the kill to be completed. You often don't even get a bank account to send payment to; contract killers have become quite finicky about this aspect of their trade as well. A lot of the payments conducted in the world of online contract killing are made via a cryptocurrency called bitcoin. Bitcoin is untraceable; only a record of the transaction remains in a series of servers called the blockchain. Hence, payment can be confirmed and the date and time is logged forever, but the identities of both parties involved can never be ascertained.

Hence, contract killing has evolved and has turned into something far bigger than it had once been. Now, contract killers are a great deal more difficult to hire, but at the same time they are much more effective at doing their jobs.

The Future

Organized crime has changed quite a bit ever since it started in the early twentieth century. One of the biggest changes that has occurred is that crime families are starting to become a great deal more democratic. Rather than being obsessed with keeping things in the family, so to speak, these crime families are starting to realize the benefits of working with a diverse range of people. Hence, contract killers are now going to change how they operate with these organized crime syndicates as well. To start off with, they are no longer going to work for a single organization. Rather, because of the fact that they are available anonymously on the dark web means that organized crime families can hire them without having to worry about liability. Since profit matters a lot more than loyalty now, crime families are going to have absolutely no qualms whatsoever about hiring somebody that does not care about the success of the clients that hired him, instead only caring about the task he has been assigned.

It is pretty clear that the way contract killing

is conducted has changed drastically and that many of the people involved in this practice are starting to expand their horizons. While the classic mob enforcer turned contract killer is certainly a thing of the past, contract killers themselves have evolved a great deal and are probably never going to be eradicated entirely.

Myths of Modern Day Contract Killing

Because of the prevalence of contract killing in popular culture and its ensuing romanticizing, the general public has a very skewed impression of what contract killers are really like. Some of the misconceptions that people have about contract killers are as follows.

Contract Killers are Sociopaths

This probably stems from the fact that contract killers have to commit several murders over the course of their careers. While it is certainly true that in order to be a contract killer with a long and successful career you need to have a certain disregard for human life, at the same time it is important to note that the vast majority of contract killers really only did this for the money.

There are definitely a few examples of contract killers that took a great deal of pleasure in the act of killing. Richard Kuklinski certainly exemplified this trait, killing far and wide for the pleasure of it and often taking contracts that were far below his standard payment so that he could feel the rush of killing. Still, his ritualistic modus operandi as well as the general pleasure he felt while completing his contracts made Kuklinski a bit of a serial killer as well. This is decidedly an anomaly in the world of contract killing.

There is a good reason why such sociopaths don't make good contract killers. People that take pleasure in the act of killing would often forget the purpose of the killing itself. They would eschew the basic goal of the contract, which is to satisfy the client's wishes, in favor of killing in a manner that is preferable to them. Additionally, the ritualistic nature in which killers-for-pleasure tend to operate makes them far more likely to be tracked. Kuklinski managed to have a long career in spite of his ritual, but once again he is an outlier here. The vast majority of contract killers that get into the business for pleasure end up getting caught because authorities are easily able to track them down by noting down the various aspects of the crime scene they find particularly intriguing.

Contract Killers are Criminal Masterminds

Movies such as Collateral tend to depict contract killers as these geniuses who are always one step ahead of everyone else. The reason for this is that people view contract killing as an intricate art that would require the skills of a ninja. This is not exactly true either. A contract killer would have to have some street smarts, and an above average level of intelligence is important if said killer wants to have a long career, but this in no way means that all contract killers are going to be geniuses.

Often, people get into contract killing because they do not have the brains for anything else. Criminal geniuses tend to go into less violent and infinitely more profitable ventures such as drug trafficking. These ventures tend to bring in a great deal more revenue which means more money can be invested into expanding the business.

This stereotype is rather ironic when you consider the fact that contract killers usually work for the real geniuses. They use their brute force, low cunning and overall willingness to inflict violence as a tool that makes them useful to mob bosses and the like, people who have a more balanced approach to crime and use their talents in much more productive ways. This also shows just how essential contract killers are to the overall criminal underworld – they're not just important for their brains, rather being considered necessary for their killing skills.

Contract Killers Earn Lots of Money

When you see a hit man or a contract killer in a movie, you would notice that they tend to have enormous, lavish homes. Often they live in Europe, have gorgeous wives and drive sports cars. This is because a lot of people assume that contract killers get paid enormous amounts of money. After all, they are being paid to kill people, right?

The logic behind this thought process is more or less sound, but the sad fact is that contract killers often don't earn that much money at all. This is because most of them work independently and are hired by people that want revenge on others rather than crime bosses. The most common reason for hiring a contract killer is wanting to collect on life insurance money. The people that usually hire contract killers don't usually have a lot of money, and so contract killers have to make do with the few hundred dollars per kill they usually get.

Contract Killers Only Work with Organized Crime

Organized crime is certainly the most visible criminal industry in which contract killing is prevalent, but the contract killers hired by these organizations and families are the absolute cream of the crop. They are the rarest contract killers in that they are ridiculously efficient at getting the job done, and more often than not they end up providing their bosses with a number of other services as well.

Most contract killers are small time. They do not get nearly as much coverage as other comparable members of their industry, but the fact of the matter remains that they are far more prevalent. The reason that people tend to think that all contract killers are highly paid mob enforcers is because these are the ones that are caught most often. They have ties to the mob and are thus high value targets, and their kill counts are usually much higher. Additionally, the people they kill are often more prominent which further makes them prime candidates for police intervention, and their name gets spoken of far more often than the average contract killer.

What you need to understand is that the vast majority of contract killers lie low and keep their heads down. They don't want to be famous or notorious; they just want to earn their money and stay out of jail. This is why so many myths about these people are completely untrue.

Vincent Coll – Mad Dog

Vincent Coll is an example of a contract killer that was active during the earliest days of modern-day organized crime in America. He quickly gained notoriety for his brutishness and his willingness to resort to violence, and his career set the path for a lot of contract killers to come, many of which would try to emulate him in some way and attempt to build on his legacy.

Early Days

Born in a small town in Ireland in 1908, Coll did not spend all that much time in his country of birth. Approximately a year after he was born, his parents decided to move to America during the initial stages of the mass immigration that Ireland was seeing in those days.

The early days of Coll's life in America were fraught with misery. His father decided that New York was the place that they should go, like many other people in those days, as this truly was the city of opportunity. Coll's family lived in the Bronx which is where he grew up, but it was a childhood spent in great poverty. A few years after the move to America, Coll's father ended up abandoning the family, which meant that Coll's mother was left to try and provide for all of her children. Six years after the family had moved to America, Coll's mother succumbed to tuberculosis. Raising several children is a very difficult task, especially if the person in question is doing it alone.

Over the next eleven years, Coll did not just end up losing his mother. Five of Coll's six siblings ended up dying as well due to his family's poor living conditions, which meant that by the time he was twelve years old, he had almost become an only child. This was particularly traumatizing because, after the death of his mother when he was eight years old, Coll's sister had taken up the task of raising him and his surviving siblings. Once most of his siblings were dead, Coll was left with just his brother Pete who became an important part of his career as a criminal later on.

A childhood spent in such conditions can have a psychological impact on a person, and this is probably the genesis of the violent urges that would later cause Vincent Coll to become a contract killer. Such dysfunctional childhoods are very commonly seen in contract killers as well as anyone who shows certain violent urges and has a tendency to be overly aggressive. The same is true for Vincent Coll.

After Coll's sister died when he was twelve, he was adopted unofficially by a woman that lived in the same area as his family had when they had been alive. This elderly woman attempted to give Coll a good upbringing by sending him to good schools and the like, but the damage had been done and it was too late now. Coll was expelled from pretty much every school he went to because he kept getting into fights.

Start of Criminal Career

Maladjusted children tend to find approval in places that are really not that healthy. However, there really is nothing that can be done for children that attempt to interact with others in this manner. The truth of the matter is that the vast majority of children with childhoods this dysfunctional tend to react to this by becoming extremely violent. Living in such squalor meant that Coll had to fight for what he wanted, no matter how small it was. Hence, this violence became more than just a way for him to release aggression. It was more than just a tool that could be brought out when there was a fight or any other situation where such aggression might be required. No, in this situation, aggression and violence became a way of life for Coll, a sign that he was no longer a child.

Coll's first arrest came at the age of twelve, the same age that he lost his sister. He was sent to a reform school, but he was so violent that he ended up getting kicked out after a rather short period of time. After several expulsions, Coll began to make a name for himself since these schools were meant for delinquents, children that did not have anyone to teach them what was the right thing to do. Hence, with his street credentials slowly starting to rise, Coll ended up joining his first street gang. This gang was called The Gophers, and while it may not have been the most high-end criminal outfit in the city, it was Coll's introduction to organized crime within a specific structure. The Gophers ended up collapsing because it was essentially just a gang of children that were messing around, but Coll learned valuable lessons while he was in this gang.

To start off with, this gang allowed him to have his first run-in with the police of the city. These run-ins taught Coll the ruthlessness of the police of the time and alienated him further, and it also taught him how to handle it if he ended up getting captured by the police. Being in this gang also played the important role of showing Coll how he could interact with his fellow gang members. It was during his tenure with this band that Coll ended up learning that unspoken criminal code that prevents people from ratting one another out. This was the beginning for Coll, and being a part of this gang helped him build an even bigger reputation, one that was well outside the closeted environment of reformatory schools. On the streets, people were starting to look at him as a very violent individual, one that was unpredictable but also had a keen mind in a lot of situations. All in all, Coll was a brute and everyone knew it. By this point in his life, he was well on his way to becoming "Mad Dog" Coll.

Professional Contract Killer Beginnings

By the time Mad Dog Coll had reached his mid-teens, he had been arrested over a dozen times for various offenses. It was at this point in his life that he truly started to become a proper criminal, one that would become legendary because of how he would spend his entire career. One aspect of his current persona is the fact that Coll was so famous for the way he dressed. He actually epitomized the old school gangster that you might typically associate criminals with because of the fact that he wore such expensive clothes. Tailored suits, a fedora which he always wore at an angle along with the finest shirts; all of these were a part of Mad Dog's wardrobe. These clothes, when juxtaposed with the extremely menacing air that Mad Dog always seemed to exude, somehow served to make him even scarier than he had been before.

It was this reputation that got Coll his first proper job as a criminal. Dutch Schultz was one of the people running crime in New York City. This was prohibition-era America, a time when alcohol was illegal, and Schultz primarily made profit by brewing and selling alcohol illegally. He needed enforcers, muscle that would be able to ensure that people paid the exorbitant prices that he asked them to pay. Coll was perfect for this job, and he also started to get hired as a contract killer by Schultz. He killed numerous people over the course of his career as a contract killer, all of which served Schultz's interest in some way. Coll was always known to be a wild card, and his problems with authority meant that it was highly unlikely that he was going to stick around with a boss for very long.

As he entered his late teens, Coll had started to amass his own following. While this following was not yet referred to a gang as it were, it was still greatly feared. In spite of the gang that he was beginning to accumulate, Coll was still beholden to Schultz, which was why it seemed like his criminal career was going to end up going nowhere. As a contract killer, he had started to get an incredible reputation, but this reputation was not the sort of thing that Schultz wanted. What he wanted was respect; he wanted people to fear him as a criminal in his own right and not just because he worked for someone that they were already afraid of.

It was at this point that Coll made his first solo robbery while working for Dutch Schultz. This robbery ended up being quite profitable, with the earnings being upwards of seventeen thousand dollars. This was close to a quarter of a million dollars if you account for inflation. This was a huge robbery for Coll, but the fact that he had performed it without his boss's blessing meant that Schultz was quite angry.

The confrontation following this robbery was the first instance of Schultz and Coll having some kind of falling out. Coll refused to be apologetic for what he had done, claiming that he had as much a right as Schultz did to rob people. He claimed that he deserved to be made a partner in Schultz's operation, but Schultz obviously refused. Coll and Schultz parted ways, and what was once a functional and respectful working relationship turned into great enmity, enmity that would result in tremendous loss of life over the next few years.

When Coll reached twenty-one years of age, he had a complete gang that was so strong that he decided to go to war with Schultz. This war was an attempt to take Schultz's territory from him, and it got very violent very fast. One of the first people that ended up getting killed during this war turned out to be Coll's older brother Pete. This caused the war to escalate even further, and by the end of it, close to two dozen men were killed. This was a period of enormous social upheaval for New York, as there were two vicious gang wars being fought at the same time.

Mad Dog's Downfall

One of Coll's techniques for earning money during this period of time was by ransoming members of mob families. It was definitely a profitable enterprise, but the one mistake that Mad Dog ended up making was that he targeted somebody at the wrong time. He was trying to take down a mid-tier level member of Schultz's gang when a stray bullet ended up hitting a child that had been playing close by. This was the beginning of the end for Coll. After the child was murdered, the police became absolutely vehement about capturing him, and a manhunt was launched. Over the course of this manhunt, Mad Dog made many attempts to disguise himself, but with his gang broken up after increased police presence following the murder of the child, Mad Dog was not left with many options, and not long after the manhunt was launched he was captured.

Although he was released on a technicality, Coll was no longer as powerful as he had once been. He turned to contract killing once again in the wake of a series of gang wars that had left a single person, Salvatore Maranzano, as the Don of all organized crime in New York City. Maranzano wanted to kill his right-hand man out of a fear that he would kill him first in order to take the top spot, a move that echoes the manner in which assassins were often used centuries ago. The amount that Coll demanded in order to do this is equal to $750,000 dollars in today's money, so it was pretty clear that Mad Dog Coll was a highly in-demand killer.

Schultz was still after Coll, and after bribing police officers and using Coll's former accomplices to ascertain his whereabouts, he had Mad Dog killed. Coll was 23 when he died, but in his short life he had already left a legacy that few, if any, would be able to live up to.

Marinko Magda – The Serbian Shooter

Marinko Magda is an example of an individual that was active outside of the United States who was extremely proficient at contract killing. Most people seem to think that contract killers in general are present in the United States and no other country, but the truth of the matter is that these individuals are present throughout the world. Magda is known to be one of the most ruthless contract killers in history, and it is because of this that he plays such an important role in the overall development of contract killers in the modern era.

One thing about Magda that stands out is the fact that there is so little known about his personal life. All that is known is that he was active in Hungary for a period of time, and that he killed well over a dozen people. He was a wild card that was known to work with a wide variety of mob bosses but was never tied to any single operation, and the major benefit of this was that he was able to branch out and ensure that he was not forced to work with any single private entity.

Magda's preferred mode of killing was a gun, but he was also known to use strangulation and the like on a regular basis in order to ensure that the subject was dead. Certain situations required him to have a much more subtle approach, and it was in these situations that he excelled. Strangulation via a wire was the sort of thing that he preferred in such situations because it allowed him to kill his targets without making any noise whatsoever. In this manner, Magda proved that he had it in him to kill pretty much anybody he chose, thus making it a great deal easier for mob bosses to rely on him to get the job done.

Another aspect of Magda's career that is very noticeable is the fact that he had an extremely approachable nature in the sense that people outside the world of organized crime also tended to opt for him when they were looking to have someone killed. He fulfilled numerous personal vendettas, and it is this facet that makes him so ruthless in the eyes of law enforcement all over the world.

The people he killed often had nothing to do with the world of organized crime in any way. Rather than being a part of this organized crime outfit, they were normal business owners and the like, people who were known to run small shops in towns surrounding his home city of Subotica in Hungary. His reputation for being brutal with his victims made him extremely feared by people living in these towns, and he earned quite a bit of money in the process. While most contract killers don't command all that great a fee at all, Magda was known to command large prices because of the fact that he was so efficient. Efficiency in all things is the sort of trait that people look for when they are trying to get someone killed so that they can rest assured that, no matter what happens, they are going to be safe from any punishment that might be inflicted if an investigation opens up in the murder cases.

One aspect of Magda's career that people often tend to forget is that he ended up getting messy towards the end of it. While he was certainly well known for how quickly he dispatched his victims, his disposal of the evidence towards this period of time became very subpar because he had started to get overconfident. In 1995 he was charged with three murders which meant that he started to serve 30 years in prison.

His violent ways did not end in prison either. Rather, Magda made a reputation for himself as the sort of person that would fight prison guards, something that the vast majority of inmates were afraid to do because it could cause serious problems for them. These problems stemmed from the mob nature of prison guards, as these individuals tend to look out for their own and treat any aggression against them very seriously indeed.

About ten years after he was sentenced, he was fined approximately 40,000 Hungarian francs for his frequent violent episodes. With twenty years in his sentence remaining, Magda was going to have to pay the amount back piece by piece. If he did not pay it back before his sentence had been served, he was going to end up serving close to an additional year in prison as further punishment. It was highly likely that he was going to end up inflicting more violence in prison, so his prison sentence was likely to increase even more.

Magda is a great example of how normal people also frequently acquire the services of a contract killer. While he did also work for a number of organized crime outfits, the fact of the matter remained that he was an extremely powerful killer that also worked for normal people, people that would have otherwise had to swallow their anger and move on. This shows an interesting dynamic, because it reveals that people are willing to pay money to have people killed just because they were slighted or because they were cheated in some way.

The people he killed include a confectioner and a nurse, showing that most of his victims were innocents that were involved in things that they did not understand. Cheating spouses, conmen and the like were also a regular part of his list of victims, which provided him with riches untold as this was just how desperate his clients were to get the revenge that they so sorely craved.

Christopher Dale Flannery- Mister Rent-a-Kill

Australia is known for its many wild animals that are incredibly dangerous and have a tendency to strike when least expected. All the same, one of the animals that Australia might not be all that well known for, since he is not actually an animal, is Christopher Dale Flannery. He is a great example of a contract killer that was never really caught. Even now his crimes are alleged ones that were never really proven, and this is all because he was so great at covering his tracks.

The key to his success is the fact that stealth was his proper motive. Stealth is the sort of thing that you really can't rate highly enough when it comes to contract killers because you are involved in something that a lot of people are going to be after you for. Perhaps Flannery's biggest example of genius is the fact that he looked so mild-mannered. If you take the example of Mad Dog Coll, you are going to notice that he had the appearance that has been popularized in media these days. In spite of this fact, a lot of the contract killers that gained a great deal of fame in later years were known instead for their tendency to blend into a crowd. If you think about it, this is the sort of thing that would help a contract killer enjoy a long and fruitful career. After all, Mad Dog Coll ended up getting killed at 23 and was known to be a contract killer, whereas Christopher Dale Flannery was never caught in the first place.

This shows the importance of blending in for a contract killer, and Flannery exemplified this trait more than anything else. Flannery displays all of the hallmarks of a contract killer that people tend to notice. He had a very disturbed childhood and did not complete his schooling. In fact, he left school when he was only fourteen years old. In spite of this fact, he was known to be very intelligent, although his intelligence was restricted more to street smarts than anything else. The true key to his success was the fact that he knew how to improvise, but this was just not the sort of thing that schools tended to favor. Rather, they preferred that individuals in this category did not take part in the schooling process at all, which was one of the biggest reasons why Flannery was not known to be all that great when it came to academics.

Once he left school, he embarked on a career in crime. This criminal career started with a few minor cases of breaking and entering, and apart from that he was known for being violent during his crimes as well. This came from his tendency to approach the very concept of crime from a violent point of view. He simply did not believe that he had the ability to complete the tasks that he was assigned without resorting to violence, so a career as a contract criminal was in a lot of ways inevitable for this individual.

His initial career as a criminal did not last very long. After three years of robbing people in violent episodes, Flannery was finally arrested when he was seventeen. Due to the violent nature of his crimes, the judge refused to be lenient with him and ended up making him serve seven whole years in prison. This is where Flannery truly started to come into his own.

Prison is the sort of environment that breaks the weak and makes the strong. Flannery was very strong indeed, which was why he excelled in prison. He got into a lot of fights, but this just won him the respect of other inmates. The contacts that he made during his bout in prison ended up serving a very important role in his career in the future, and it allowed him to get clients that would hire him to do killings on their behalf.

During his seven years in prison, he was known for not really taking sides when it came to gangs. Even though the vast majority of inmates tended to be extremely particular about which gang they ended up siding with, since this was the sort of thing that would allow them to survive in prison, Flannery was a lot more ad hoc about the whole thing. In spite of his rather violent streak, he was also known to be quite diplomatic when it came to gang relations, which allowed him to not take any sides, thereby enabling him to enjoy a much more fruitful career in the future. The fact that he did not take any sides allowed him to get clients from any criminal organization, since none of them ended up getting alienated during his stint in jail when he made all of the contacts that he would use in the future.

Following his seven-year stint in jail, Flannery was released and he ended up becoming a bouncer at a strip club. Directionless and with nowhere to really go and nothing to show for the way he had lived his life up until this point in time, Flannery decided to act on the offers that he had gotten in prison and took up contract killing. This really allowed him to come into his own as a criminal, simply because of the fact that he was so good at what he did.

When he started contract killing, he mostly

focused on smaller hits initially. This is because he was inexperienced and the people that were hiring him knew how violent he was and were reluctant to hand him any of their bigger targets just yet. Flannery was also known to take very small amounts of money in order to complete the task. Whether this was because he did not have the education necessary in order to understand how much his skills were worth or because the pleasure of killing was enough for him is not known, much like there is very little else that is known about this person.

Over the years, Flannery settled down and married. He had children as well, and none of his family members knew about the fact that he was a cold-blooded killer that frequently killed people in order to earn as much money as possible. The major drawback of this was that when the police started to track him down and learn as much as they could about him, his family was not able to back him up.

However, as has been mentioned before, Flannery was exceedingly good at hiding his tracks, and he was able to use this talent to ensure that he was never convicted of anything. The two times that he did go to trial, he was acquitted on technicalities as well as a lack of evidence. This meant that Flannery was free from jail, but it also meant that there was a lot of heat on him, and heat meant that the people that he usually worked with would no longer be willing to hire him. Seeing no end to the police investigation due to the fact that they were convinced of his guilt, he decided that he would leave his family behind and opt for a fresh start. This fresh start ended up being in Sydney.

After hiding in Sydney for a time and lying low, Flannery began contract killing yet again. This time his rates were a lot higher than what they had once been. The reason for this was that he had developed a reputation for himself, and at the same time, he had started to realize that his talents were worth far more money than he was charging at this point in time. This was a sign that Flannery was growing up and that he was starting to make himself into the contract killer that everyone expected him to be.

His success in Sydney was not meant to last. He had made a lot of enemies over his career, because as a contract killer there was only so long that one could be diplomatic and play all sides. Flannery was asked by his boss to meet him, and this was the last time that he was ever heard from. After he left from the meeting, he was seen getting into a taxi, but after this point, nobody ever found out what happened to him.

All of the details regarding his murders come from people that spoke up after he disappeared. It is highly likely that if he had remained active, he would not have been caught for quite some time. Due to the mysterious nature of his disappearance as well as the severity of the violence that he inflicted upon others, Flannery has become an important part of Australian pop culture, with a number of shows and documentaries about him airing.

Cold Blooded Professional Killers
Abdullah Catli

Although in the modern day, contract killers were rarely used to kill for overtly political motives, Catli is an example of how many contract killers were used as weapons by the state. He was an ultra-nationalist and an advocate for far right policies, and the government of Turkey, the country he hailed from, used his talents many times over in order to silence people that were left of center.

Catli was used time and time again in order to prevent rebellions from occurring and keep the population subdued. This led to him having one of the most prolific victim counts in the history of contract killing. Usually, a killer with forty kills is considered to be respectable, someone that has a fair bit of experience and knows what he is doing since he was able to kill this many people without getting caught. Someone that has killed four hundred is an absolute legend, the sort of contract killer whose name is spoken in hushed whispers in case he might be listening in. Hundreds of kills turns you into a bogeyman that practically every single person in the criminal underworld would be afraid of.

Catli killed over four thousand people, and the number might even be higher than that. What's more, he was not a mass murderer. He killed specific targets that were deemed to be threats to the state, which means that he killed almost one person a day over the course of his career. This level of prolific killing is truly unheard of, and it shows that Catli was truly one of the most cold-blooded contract killers out there. After all, someone that can kill thousands of people has to be either insane or utterly amoral.

John Childs

If you have read up on contract killers, you know that they are some of the most brutal, violent individuals that you could possibly imagine. Yet, few of them would go so far as to harm a child. John Childs, on the other hand, was the sort of killer who had no qualms whatsoever about killing children. He did not mind killing elderly people either. He was often hired to kill entire families specifically for this reason, which is why his reputation as a killer allowed him to earn so much money.

The general process of his murders involved killing his victim, cutting them into little pieces, and then using a mincing machine to make these little parts finer still. He would then incinerate the remains of his victims in his fireplace, leaving absolutely no evidence for police to find.

Childs was also known for the brutal manner in which he killed his victims. He was often known to use a hammer, a weapon that could cause a slow, violent and very painful death. The pleasure he took in killing isolated him from most people since he gave off a vibe that tended to put other people off.

Stretko Kalinic

A contract killer kills for money. There is usually no other factor involved. But, you do have a few contract killers that are in this business for the fun of it. Kalinic was one such individual. He often didn't even ask for payment when he was given a target to kill, preferring to murder people as a way of giving his friends favors.

He was part of a highly violent and sadistic gang in Eastern Europe. Kalinic's presence in this gang is both the reason why it saw such a meteoric rise as well as the reason it came crashing down in such a short period of time. This is because Kalinic's brutality first served as a way to intimidate rival gangs but then became a modus operandi that was easy to trace because Kalinic left a lot of saliva on his victims. After all, he often ate them.

To this day, there have been no other contract killers that went so far as to cannibalize their victims. The extremes that Kalinic went to show that he was an entirely different breed of contract killer, far more violent than any that came before or have come since.

Bernard Hunwick

Hunwick was widely known for his wild partying lifestyle, the fact that he was married to a Playboy bunny, as well as the fact that he could turn pretty much any object into an explosive. He used this skill quite a few times over the course of his career, creating bombs that were specifically meant to cause pain.

As a result of his ingenuity, he ended up

giving hundreds of people extremely painful deaths. He was known to enjoy watching his victims suffering, something that almost got him caught numerous times and resulted in a traceable pattern that eventually led the police back to him.

In spite of the fact that Hunwick killed hundreds of people, the police were only able to prove a single murder. This ended up sending him to jail, so at least he was not able to kill anyone ever again.

Jimmy Moody

Generally, contract killers that are extremely bombastic and attract a lot of attention tend not to last very long. This makes the case of Jimmy Moody quite interesting, because he tended to attract enormous amounts of attention to himself, but in spite of this, his career lasted decades. While he did do a few stints in prison, they were never so long that his career was put in jeopardy.

Over the course of his career, Moody conducted hits for all kinds of organizations. The thing that set him apart was his ability to customize kills based on the preferences of his clients. This meant that he could be brazen with his kills in order to spread panic, and he also had the potential to kill with stealth. Although he preferred the latter, Moody was great at covering his tracks as well. His long career came to an end when he was gunned down by enemies at a pub.

Charles Harrelson – Natural Born Killer

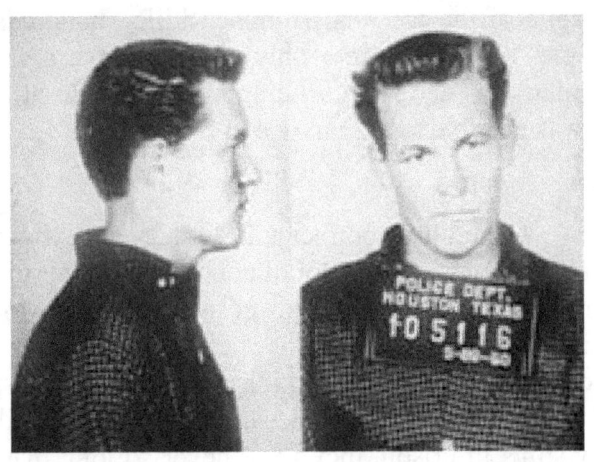

Woody Harrelson is a widely known and largely celebrated actor who made his debut on the TV show Cheers around the same time that Christopher Dale Flannery went missing. One thing that a lot of people don't know about him is the fact that he is the son of a contract killer, in fact, one of the most prominent contract killers of the latter half of the 20th century. His father's name was Charles Harrelson.

Life Before Crime

Harrelson was born in Texas in 1938. The city of Lovelady was his hometown, and he did not leave it for quite some time. He eventually moved to California where he met his future wife, the woman who would become Woody Harrelson's mother.

During this period of his life, Harrelson was involved in a number of criminal activities. Armed robbery was one of his fortes, an aspect of his criminal career that frequently goes unreported due to the fact that it is really not all that glamorous, although it did play an important role in getting him the contacts he would need to go on to experience success in his later years as a contract killer.

As for his occupation, Harrelson worked the rather mundane job of an encyclopedia salesman. The fact that he had the ability to blend into such an everyman job was one of the biggest reasons why Harrelson was successful as a contract killer. After all, someone that comes to your house to sell encyclopedias usually has a boring personality as his worst character trait. One doesn't usually expect someone so mundane to be a killer, or have it in him to cause harm to anyone.

Harrelson was also a frequent gambler. In fact, the genesis of his criminal career came from his need to pay off gambling debts which were quickly starting to get higher and higher. Eventually, the debts got so high that Harrelson was unable to manage even with the robberies that he was conducting, so he had to move on to something that would pay a great deal more, something like contract killing.

The Beginning of His Contract Killing

Harrelson had made contacts in the criminal underworld, thanks to his gambling habit. His hits were often made for mob bosses that he owed money to, although there were many occasions where he would do the hit for profit rather than to pay off a debt once his career started to take off. There were a great many individuals that he killed for profit, but one of his earliest kills was of a carpet salesman named Alan Berg. He was definitely one of Harrelson's less prominent victims, but his tale is definitely one that can be seen echoing throughout the history of contract killers.

The reasons behind Alan Berg being killed are rather mysterious, and Harrelson refused to comment on it for the remainder of his life, but many people have speculated that the hit was conducted in order to take vengeance against this person's father who had fought with a few people that turned out to have criminal ties.

The next known kill that Harrelson was hired for is similarly low key. He was paid around two thousand dollars to kill an individual by the name of Sam Degelia. Unlike the murder of Alan Berg, the reasons behind Harrelson being hired to kill Degelia are actually quite clear cut. Degelia owned a grain distribution business with his partner Peter Scamardo. Scamardo hired Harrelson to kill his partner so that he could collect on his life insurance, although it is possible that a great deal of personal enmity existed between the two as well. Hiring a contract killer in order to collect on a life insurance policy is actually quite common; in fact, it is one of the most common instances where contract killers are hired outside of organized crime syndicates. This is one of the murders that resulted in Harrelson's eventual downfall, although there were several more widely publicized murders later on that would really seal his fate.

Following a police investigation, evidence of foul play was discovered, which led to the authorities arresting Harrelson. This was the first time that his status as a contract killer came to light. In 1968, Harrelson went on trial for the murder of Degelia. Yet, due to an indecisive jury, he ended up getting let off the hook, and his successful murder of Degelia, along with his avoidance of suffering the consequences for his actions, led to him becoming highly in demand. The Degelia murder would come back to haunt him later on, however, for the next five years, he was free to continue his career and gain even more notoriety for the efficiency with which he fulfilled his contracts and the cold, precise nature of his kills.

In 1973, the case was reopened and Harrelson was tried once again. This time his machinations and cunning were insufficient to prevent him from getting a guilty verdict, and for this crime, Harrelson was sentenced to fifteen years in a maximum security prison. In spite of the fact that he had killed someone in cold blood, Harrelson managed to get released early from prison due to his inherent understanding of the prison system and how it works. He behaved impeccably while incarcerated, avoiding gang politics and the fights that ensue as a result of these politics and kept his head low. As a result, in seven years he was out on the streets again, free to continue his once again thriving career.

His previous successes had left Harrelson overconfident, and shortly after his parole, he ended up taking on a contract that would be his end. It was a highly lucrative contract because it involved the murder of a visible public figure, an individual by the name of John H. Wood, a district judge who was set to try a notorious drug kingpin named Jamiel Chagra. Wood was known for providing extremely harsh sentences to the people he was set to judge, so in order to preserve his freedom and nudge the legal system towards calling a mistrial, Chagra hired Harrelson to take the judge out.

Harrelson was successful in killing the judge, but he did not manage to escape the long arm of the law this time around because of an anonymous tip. To this day, the identity of this tipper is unknown, but this was the final nail in Harrelson's coffin. Following the tip, police were able to obtain a recorded conversation that Chagra had with his imprisoned brother, a conversation that described in detail how he was intending to have the judge killed in order to avoid his trial.

With all of the evidence stacked against him, Harrelson was sentenced to consecutive life sentences in the year 1979. He consistently claimed that he had not killed the judge and had instead only taken credit for the act so that he would be able to secure payment from Chagra. Chagra's testimony proved that Harrelson was indeed the person to pull the trigger and kill the judge.

Harrelson stayed in prison for twenty-five years during which he reconnected with his now famous son, although his son remained reluctant to call this man his father. In the year 1995, he attempted an escape for which he was sent to a supermax prison where he was no longer allowed to have any visitors. Harrelson died of cardiac arrest in the year 2007, but the letters that he had sent to his family indicated that he had managed to find some small measure of peace during his final stint in prison. Perhaps he was happy that he was no longer in the game, because the life of a contract killer seems to inevitably attract said individual to a life of crime time and time again.

A Charming Personality

One of the aspects of Harrelson's personality that gave him great success as a contract killer was the fact that he was so charming. He was not at all brutish like the last few contract killers that have been mentioned in this book. Rather, he was known to be extremely articulate, and he was also an avid reader, having read hundreds of books while he was in prison. It was his well-read nature that allowed him to blend into the crowd, the mark of a successful contract killer.

His contract killing career was comprised of a number of different attacks on several people. Most of his victims were quite prominent, with Harrelson targeting low-level politicians most of all. While these were his more prominent victims, Harrelson was also widely known to kill regular people as well as long as the price was right. He generally charged around two thousand dollars in order to kill someone that was not that prominent, with the price going up quite a bit if the target was not the sort of person that could be easily accessed.

Richard Kuklinski – The Iceman

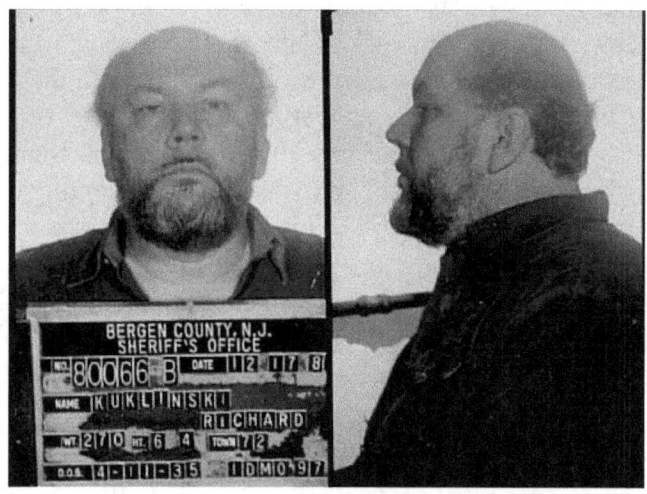

If there is one individual that fits the bill of an iconic contract killer, it is Richard Kuklinski. In his long career spanning decades, Kuklinski killed many people for a variety of criminal organizations. One notable aspect of Kuklinski's career is the fact that he did not kill people outside the criminal underworld, which meant that he did not kill people for insurance claims or in order to fulfill someone's personal vendetta. He was a highly paid contract killer throughout his career, and his notoriety was such that an entire film was made about him which accurately depicted the fact that he successfully balanced a double life as a married family man and a contract killer until the moment he was caught.

Early Life

Kuklinski was born in New Jersey to immigrant parents, both of whom were very religious. This resulted in his strict Catholic upbringing which he frequently tried to rebel against, resulting in the ire of his abusive mother as well as his father who often resorted to physical violence. This abusive upbringing desensitized Kuklinski and made him accepting of violence as a way of life. This facet of his personality really allowed him to succeed as a contract killer, since he had no qualms about killing people at all, and there is reason to believe that he, in fact, took great pleasure in the act of killing.

Although his history of violence extends all the way into his teenage years when he beat a child in his neighborhood to death for trying to bully him. To the people in his life, Kuklinski always seemed like a stand-up guy who would never hurt a fly. This ability to seamlessly hide that aspect of his life enabled him to enjoy a longer career as a contract killer than most people tend to have, and it also allowed him to enjoy the pleasure of raising a family for several years. While neighbors and friends had no idea that Kuklinski had violent tendencies, let alone had an inkling about the fact that he killed people for money, his wife stated after his incarceration that he was frequently physically abusive towards her. This can be attributed to his own upbringing where the people that were supposed to care for him were the ones that caused him grief. This dynamic certainly impacted Kuklinski in a major way and made him incapable of the emotional attachments that other people tend to take for granted.

Before he turned to a life of crime, Kuklinski was a blue collar worker who was just getting by. It is not quite known whether it was a need for money that made him take up the mantle of a contract killer or the fact that he wanted to release some of the pent-up aggression that he had built up over the course of his childhood. The only thing that people truly know is the fact that Kuklinski spent many years killing out of anger or revenge, but at the same time did not profit from his talents for a significant period of time.

The Start of His Career

In an attempt to boost his financial status, Kuklinski began to work with a criminal syndicate known as the Gambino crime family. He initially worked as an enforcer, inflicting vengeance upon those that failed or refused to pay protection money. His efficiency as an enforcer made the mob that he worked for hire him as a contract killer quite quickly, and he took to this job like a fish to water.

After his incarceration, Kuklinski claimed that he killed hundreds of people over the course of his criminal career. The veracity of this information has not been verified, but the people that he was proved to have killed are so great in number that it is very possible that Kuklinski could be telling the truth.

As for his modus operandi, Kuklinski was

generally not all that picky about the weapon that he used. He preferred guns in general, but he was also known to use knives if the need arose. His versatility was one of the biggest reasons why he was in such high demand throughout his career, because different situations tend to require different approaches. One aspect of his modus operandi that remained consistent, in fact, almost ritualistic, was the fact that he froze his victims in order to preserve their bodies after he had killed them. This is what lead to him getting the nickname of Iceman, although many also suggest that it could have been because of how cold blooded he was and how he never shied away from any kind of violence.

He generally froze the people he killed as a forensic countermeasure. This is an interesting aspect of Kuklinski's MO because it indicates that he had a sharp criminal mind and was not just the sort of person that had violence in his mind and little else. The freezing process made it virtually impossible to tell when the victim had been killed, thus making the job of the police investigating these murders infinitely more difficult.

Nevertheless, it must also be noted that the almost ritualistic nature of Kuklinski's freezing of his victims might be seen as a sign of serial killer tendencies in this contract killer. While the vast majority of contract killers only killed for money, the prolific nature of Kuklinski's victim list makes it very possible that he had certain psychological aspects common in a number of serial murderers. He is known as a contract killer, however, and the serial killer theory only arose several years after his conviction when he began to talk about his killings and his personality was examined by behavioral analysis experts. An additional aspect of Kuklinski's criminal career that also often goes unnoticed is the fact that his crimes were not restricted to murder. Kuklinski was involved in a number of different criminal activities that made him famous in the criminal underworld.

A Diverse Range of Crimes

Once Kuklinski had established a name for himself as a highly efficient contract killer, his criminal career opened up quite a bit. The various criminal organizations that he worked for needed people to provide them with a variety of services in order to expand their operations, and since Kuklinski was known to be dependable, his entry into these differing criminal fields was inevitable.

One of the first criminal industries that Kuklinski started to participate in was the selling of illegal drugs. Heroin was his mainstay; serving as an enforcer would ensure that people that bought heroin from these criminal organizations would pay up on time. In addition to heroin, he was known to sell crystal meth as well as cocaine, and by acquiring his services, criminal organizations were able to greatly increase their influence, thereby ensuring that they would have consistent cash flow which resulted in a greater influx of crime in that area.

In this manner, Kuklinski became an intrinsic part of the criminal community in his home town as well as surrounding areas. This was another important aspect of his career because it ended up creating newer opportunities for him, opportunities that might have not otherwise arisen.

The drug game was not the area of criminal activity outside of contract killing that Kuklinski excelled in. His preferred activity was the selling of arms and weapons, since this business attracted his more violent side. He made a lot of profit in this business and became a respected arms dealer in his own right. An interesting thing to note here is that, even though Kuklinski had become a successful criminal that was earning a great deal of money during the peak of his career, he continued his contract killing work as well, even though this did not pay as much. Competing theories try to explain this behavior, but one of the most popular theories states that Kuklinski enjoyed the process of contract killing so much that he just could not bring himself to part with these jobs. Since the lack of legal enforcement of killing contracts made it hard to find trustworthy people in the criminal underworld, mob bosses and the like were more than happy to keep giving Kuklinski more work in this area since they knew that he would always deliver on his contracts and that he was not going to complain about how difficult a particular kill was going to be for him.

A Different Kind of Contract Killer

Perhaps the most intriguing aspect of Kuklinski's career as a criminal is how much he enjoyed contract killing. The vast majority of contract criminals, while inherently violent and not perturbed by the nature of their occupations in any way, did not actually enjoy killing others. Rather, they treated their contracts like any other freelancer would, as an opportunity to earn money and nothing else.

The fact that Kuklinski froze his victims after killing them also makes it difficult to classify Kuklinski as a contract killer and nothing more. Though this was a forensic countermeasure, during his last few years as a contract killer, Kuklinski had started to make a lot of mistakes. He started leaving evidence at the scenes of his crimes and forgot to kill people that might have ended up testifying against him. And yet, in spite of the sloppiness that had come with his overconfidence and belief in his own invincibility, Kuklinski still froze his victims. By this point, this was no longer a forensic countermeasure. Rather, it was a part of Kuklinski's ritual, an aspect of his killing that made the whole process all the more enjoyable for him and allowed him to feel a sense of completion whenever he successfully fulfilled the terms of his contract.

Because of the ritualistic nature of Kuklinski's killings, a lot of people claim that he can be classified as a serial killer. While he was not known to kill purely for pleasure outside of contracts for which he was getting paid, it is also important to note that the payments he was getting were no longer necessary since Kuklinski was earning good money from his other criminal operations as well. The unusually large list of victims that Kuklinski frequently boasted about is also proof that he is not quite like other people that worked in his profession.

A Straight Edged Man

In spite of the fact that Kuklinski was a criminal who had no qualms about violence, he was actually quite a straight edge when compared to his peers and contemporaries. Kuklinski did not drink, smoke or do any drugs, and he was not known to sleep around, rather preferring to remain faithful to his wife.

This further increases how interesting Kuklinski seems to people. When you think of a criminal, you think of a person that is despicable in pretty much every way. You do not expect to read about a man that stays faithful to his wife. After all, when you murder people for money, morality is pretty much out the window.

Kuklinski's career as a contract killer started out as a way to earn money and improve his social status, and it evolved into a way for him to release the inexplicable but incessant aggression and anger that he felt at the world around him. Though his violence did affect the people closest to him, people like his wife and his children who he was frequently physically violent with, this was still not enough to tip people off about his double life since there are millions of men around the world that are abusive towards their families, yet they would never kill anyone for money.

Kuklinski is perhaps one of the most intriguing contract killers to ever be talked about in the industry, which is why he has been the subject of so many books and documentaries and even had a successful feature film created about his life.

Alexander Solonik – Agent 47

Now that a number of American contract killers have been discussed, it is time to move on to a country that is similarly influential on a global stage, namely Russia. Russia's history of contract killings is just as sordid as America's, although their mass media tends not to glorify these individuals the way that Americans often do. Solonik's story echoes that of the majority of contract killers, with contacts made in prison providing him with the opportunity to move forward and start a career using his talent for murder and profiting a great deal due to his ability to get the job done no matter what the circumstances.

Early Life

Solonik's early life was not marked by as much poverty as a lot of the contract killers that have been discussed before, but he did show a penchant for violence that is common amongst all individuals who choose this profession. From a very young age, Solonik loved weapons and other items that could cause harm to other people. This obsession led to him becoming ostracized in his community and, as a result of this, Solonik grew up without many friends.

The relationships we have during the early years of our lives are essential to helping us develop empathy skills, and since Solonik did not have many relationships in which he was accepted, due to his parents' strict attitude as well as his antisocial behavior, he grew up to become a rather cold-blooded individual.

Another aspect of Solonik's personality that certainly contributed a great deal to his future as a contract killer was his inability to function in normal environments. He was not very good at school in spite of the fact that he had a sharp mind and was not exactly unintelligent. This was because he had a different kind of mindset from the vast majority of people that he interacted with. It is safe to say that Solonik was just not the kind of individual that would have been able to adapt to a normal life, which is why a career in crime was inevitable for this person.

Military Career

Since Solonik was an ardent fan of weaponry and most mainstream jobs were unsuitable for someone as socially inept as he was, Solonik ended up joining the military after school. Although he was conscripted, which essentially meant that he did not have an option but to serve, he approached this new career with gusto, although he chafed at the rules and regulations that he was forced to follow on a regular basis. During his time with the military, Solonik received training that allowed him to streamline his strengths as a killer. He learned how to use stealth, he learned how to use his strength efficiently, and he also learned the best ways to kill a man.

In spite of his abrasive personality, Solonik managed to get through his military career without too much of a hitch. This resulted in him getting a recommendation from his superior officer, one that allowed him to get a job as a police officer once his tenure with the army had ended. The problem was that Solonik was often too violent with the people he was apprehending. He was often antagonistic towards people that he interrogated, and he often used violent and unconstitutional tactics during his interrogations. This meant that his career as a police officer did not last very long. Soon he was discharged and, because of the blemish that this placed on his record, Solonik was not able to get an adequate, high-paying job ever again in spite of his army experience.

Since he did not have the sort of personality

that allowed him to work with other people, Solonik ended up getting a job that allowed him to stay isolated from other people. This was a job as a gravedigger at a local cemetery. The fact that he was surrounded by corpses throughout his tenure at this cemetery is rather prophetic, and it seemed to be a right fit for Solonik. He was consistently unhappy during this period because he was not earning all that much money, and he was forced to cut down on his expenses a great deal.

This was also a period of attempted emotional growth for Solonik. Now that he had a stable job that he was unlikely to get fired from, he ended up dating for a short period and married his first wife. The relationship bore him a daughter, but because of Solonik's frequent and largely unpredictable violent episodes, he was unable to make the relationship last. As a result, his wife divorced him and took custody of his daughter. In spite of Solonik's repeated efforts to gain visitation rights so that he could have a relationship with his child, his violent personality which was now a matter of public record meant that he was not given this privilege by the judge that had been assigned his case. As a result, Solonik was once again left alone without any meaningful relationships. This further isolated him and accentuated his already antisocial personality, something that would play an important role in the years to come.

A few years after his first wife had left him, Solonik married again. This marriage was slightly more stable, but the reason for this is rather sinister.

Because Solonik had so much pent-up aggression and he knew that if he took it out on his wife he would lose her as well as the son that he had gotten out of their relationship, he became a serial rapist. He took his violent urges out on other women, although he did not kill them because he knew that this would be a far more difficult thing to cover up.

While his relationship remained fairly stable, although his wife did notice that Solonik was frequently cold and distant towards her and she was suspicious of the fact that he was gone for such extended periods of time, he ended up getting sloppy and leaving evidence that led to his arrest in the year 1987. After a quick trial where the evidence was stacked against him, Solonik was convicted of rape and sentenced to eight years in prison. The rather lenient sentence was because Solonik did not have a public history of sexual violence, and since the evidence was only collected from a single victim, the judge decided to go easy on him.

In an attempt to prevent his incarceration, Solonik tried to use a final meeting with his wife as an excuse to escape. Although the attempt was initially successful with Solonik escaping the building that he was being held in before getting transferred to prison, his life as a man on the run was rather short lived. A few months after his escape, Solonik was apprehended by the authorities. He had not managed to get far because he did not have the funds to make a quick getaway.

Incarceration and Beginning of Career

Once Solonik was arrested yet again, he was taken to prison to serve his sentence. During the first couple of years that Solonik was imprisoned, he was put in solitary confinement. Partly because of his history of violence, the prison authorities did not want someone hot headed starting fights in the prison courtyard, and also because he had been a police officer. Police generally don't fare all that well in jail, because criminals automatically have a vendetta against them which eventually leads to their death.

Due to a lack of available space, Solonik ended up getting transferred to general population where he was supposed to serve the remaining six years of his sentence. He was immediately in danger, with inmates figuring out quite quickly that he had once been a cop. Solonik was able to keep himself safe by earning the respect of his fellow inmates. He did so by fending off every attack that was thrown his way, fighting off up to a dozen men at a time.

He made several criminal contacts over the next two years, after which he escaped. This time, his escape was a lot more successful. His contacts in prison promised him work on the outside, and this was when Solonik was hired as a contract killer for the first time. Since his fellow inmates had seen how brutal and cold blooded Solonik tended to be, they sent word to their criminal superiors on the outside that there was someone that could be hired to fix a variety of problems that they might be facing.

While he initially started contract killing in his home town, he was so good at it that he became highly in demand in a very short period of time. His reputation soared, thanks to the fact that he quickly dispatched any rivals that the mob had, and he did so in such a manner that nobody was able to find any evidence that could have led to an arrest. An individual that can take people out so quickly whilst insulating his employers from any legal liability is pretty much the epitome of what a professional contract killer was supposed to be, and as a result of his immense skill, Solonik found himself getting offers from a variety of people, all of whom were willing to pay him far more money than he was able to earn in his small home town.

This prompted him to move to Moscow, both the official capital of Russia as well as its crime capital, in order to find more lucrative contracts. He was attached to a single criminal organization, the Kurgan mob family, and he thrived in their criminal dynamic. By using his unique skills as a killer, Solonik was able to really boost the status of his crime family, and soon they went from a barely known outfit to a highly feared syndicate that was on par with some of the most established crime families in the country.

By eliminating rival mob bosses, Solonik secured a lot of territory for his own syndicate, and soon he was one of the highest ranked individuals in the entire family. Once he attained this status, he no longer killed for money, although this did not mean that he stopped killing entirely. Solonik was still very willing to use violence as a tool to get his enemies to back down, and he often used his skills as a killer to take revenge on people that tried to move into his territory.

Upon acquiring the top spot in the criminal organization, a rather impressive feat for someone that did not come from a criminal background, Solonik quickly became one of the most wanted men in the country. Because of the fact that he was so brutal and his crimes resulted in so much pain and suffering, authorities put a lot of effort into trying to apprehend him. In 1994, Solonik was arrested in a shootout that resulted in him being severely injured.

He was quickly put on trial, convicted and imprisoned. But, this time around, his prison sentence did not last very long at all. Not even a year after Solonik was sent to jail, he managed to escape, thanks to the help of a prison guard that was on the payroll of the mob. This prison guard gave Solonik the tools he needed to escape, thereby allowing him to get away in the dead of night when nobody was expecting it.

After he escaped, Solonik was in an even better position than before. The first time he escaped, he had nothing, which meant that he quickly got captured. The second escape was made with a better plan, and Solonik quickly found gainful, if illegal, employment. When he escaped prison a third time, he had immense resources at his disposal. Solonik was one of the most notorious men in Russia, and his face could be seen on wanted posters all across the country. All of the places that he might have been able to hide were being monitored, and he only very narrowly escaped getting apprehended several times. In spite of all of these problems, Solonik did not get captured again after his third escape from prison. His career as a contract killer had resulted in him earning far more money than he was able to spend, and once he branched out into drugs and prostitution, his wealth increased even more. This meant that Solonik was able to get a fake passport made, one that he used to flee the country.

This was a very powerful move, as it meant that the authorities were completely helpless to track him. Solonik had enjoyed a very successful career as a contract killer and mobster in Russia, but it was now time for him to move on to greener pastures.

Establishing a Syndicate in Greece

Solonik was now on the run, but his mob had contacts all over the world, including in Greece. He also had the money to lie low until the heat was off, and during this time, Solonik started to plan the rest of his career. He was an extremely experienced mobster now, one that had proven his worth time and time again. He decided to use his experience and skills to establish himself in Greece.

Within two years, Solonik managed to create a powerful crime syndicate from nothing in Greece. His new crime family was involved in several different rackets, but the two rackets that they specialized in the most were drugs and, of course, contract killing. Solonik had decided to go back to his roots and do something that he was good at. He created a hierarchical system where prospective clients could hire killers based on their budget, and the services he provided were so efficient that pretty soon crime families from all over the world were desperate to hire someone from his gang. Solonik himself sat at the very top of the hierarchy, with his rates so high that only the richest criminals in the world were able to afford hiring him to conduct a hit.

Solonik managed the two areas of his criminal empire brilliantly. To start off with, he managed his drug sales in Greece very efficiently, creating a running cash flow that kept his empire functioning and allowed Solonik to buy a lot of real estate in Athens which he used to launder his money. While his drug business thrived in Greece, the contract killing arm of his empire was similarly successful. He took a cut from each of the payments that were made to the people he employed, and he also managed to secure highly lucrative contracts for himself.

Solonik is one of the rare examples of a truly global hitman. His professionalism meant that he conducted kills all over Europe, and before the abrupt end to his career that was coming shortly, he had started to set his eyes on America as well where he knew he could double his profits, thanks to the prevalence of highly wealthy criminals in that country.

His success was highly measured. Solonik never left any evidence again, and this meant that even when the Russian authorities found out that he was living in Greece they were unable to do anything, thanks to favorable extradition laws. Since he had left no evidence of crimes in Greece, the most wanted man in Russia could not be arrested by Greek authorities either, which resulted in him becoming very secure in his business dealings. His third arrest turned out to be his last. For the rest of his criminal career, no authority was able to come close to apprehending Solonik ever again. Even though he was insulated from the threat of police capturing him, Solonik was still not completely invincible.

The Death of Agent 47

Solonik had developed code names for every contract killer that was under his employ. His employees were given agent numbers which were the terms used when they were being hired, as their names were always kept a complete secret. Solonik chose the moniker of Agent 47 for himself. He chose a number this random possibly to avoid getting caught. Naming himself Agent 1 would have made it too obvious, after all.

It was in Italy that Solonik's highly profitable career as a contract killer and a mob boss finally came to an end. He had been hired to kill a highly influential person, whose identity is still not known to this day, along with the identity of the person that hired Solonik. Although the exact details of what happened were never ascertained, Solonik was found dead. He had been strangled and there was evidence of a fight, but since Solonik was found in a dumpster, there was no way to figure out where he actually died.

Although he did not have any papers on him that would have helped police identify him, Alexander Solonik was such a notorious figure that police recognized him pretty much as soon as they saw him. Once the authorities found out he was dead, an emergency order was issued and all of Solonik's properties were seized. Upon conducting raids, police found a number of illegal items in these places. The presence of hundreds of firearms indicated that Solonik might have been thinking of expanding into arms sales, and police discovered that he sold all kinds of drugs from heroin to cocaine to crystal meth.

This was the end of Solonik's criminal empire. He is one of the most prominent hitmen in history because he managed to do so much in such a short period of time. Solonik is one of the few examples of hitmen and contract killers that went beyond their original occupations and saw upward movement while they were at the peak of their criminal careers. His persistence and professionalism made him a highly legendary figure in the criminal underworld which is why he is still talked about so often in criminal circles today.

Giuseppe Greco – The Goodfella

When one thinks of organized crime, the Sicilian Mafia tends to come to mind more than any other criminal organization. This is partly because of their frequent portrayal in popular culture with films such as The Godfather and Goodfellas having Mafiosi as their protagonists, but another important factor to consider is the fact that they are definitely one of the more prominent criminal outfits in the world.

Hence, contract killers hired by the Sicilian Mafia are going to be very interesting to study. They are definitely prevalent and have been so since the early days of the modern rendition of the Mafia, and one of the most famous examples of the Sicilian hit man is Giuseppe Greco. He was known for his loyalty to his crime family. Another aspect of his personality that was notable is that he was not as maladjusted as a lot of contract killers tend to be. Greco was known to be violent, which is an obvious trait that pretty much every contract killer tended to possess, but he was not as cold blooded as some of the killers mentioned above. This is a rather interesting thing to note when you take into consideration the fact that Giuseppe Greco is one of the most prolific contract killers of all time.

Early Life

Greco was born in Palermo, a town known for being the place of birth of a number of criminals, all of which went on to find great success in the Cosa Nostra, the Sicilian Mafia. Although the Greco family was involved in crime all around Palermo and was widely considered to be the dominant crime syndicate in that particular territory, Giuseppe did not show any interest in criminal activities during the early stages of his life. In fact, he excelled at his studies, scoring particularly high marks in ancient languages.

As time passed, the pressure of his family duties began to mount, so in order to please the people that he had grown up with and those that raised him, Giuseppe decided to join the family as an enforcer. In spite of his initial hesitance to be involved in his family's criminal activities, Greco proved himself to be quite the criminal. His rise in the criminal organization was nothing short of meteoric, gaining one of the highest ranking posts in the organization at the tender age of twenty-seven. Three years before he had even reached thirty years of age, Greco was second only to his uncle Michele who was the don of the crime family.

Initial Career

The Grecos were so influential that they had frequent dealings with the immensely powerful and widely notorious Corleone crime family, a criminal organization that was respected and feared by all but a choice few Mafia families. After a period of uneasy peace, war broke out between the major crime families, and since the Grecos were aligned with the Corleones, Giuseppe was forced to take part in this war.

The fighting lasted two years, but thanks to Greco's innate ability to find the enemy that his bosses were having trouble with and take care of him, the Corleones ended up becoming the victors. This made them the kings of Sicilian crime in general, and they ran the Cosa Nostra like a well-oiled machine. Greco was rewarded for his faithful service and became a contract killer for the Corleones, slowly leaving behind his roots and starting to work for the top family instead.

Though his earlier kills were a little sloppy, since Greco was not known to be the most careful of individuals, after receiving training from some of the older contract killers that were now retired, he slowly improved his technique until his modus operandi insulated him from any potential action that the police might have taken against him.

Ascension to Don Status

Giuseppe's work with the Corleones ended making him powerful enough to supplant his uncle and become the leader of the Greco crime family. He did this by creating an image for himself as the face of the future. His uncle's policies were widely considered to be lacking in a certain aggression, and the Grecos certainly resented the fact that they had not managed to increase their influence and were seemingly content with picking up whatever leftovers the Corleones left them with.

After securing the support of the vast majority of younger Mafiosi in his family, Giuseppe planned a successful coup. His uncle gave up quite quickly, realizing that there was nothing he could do at this point to prevent the worst case scenario from occurring. Michele was allowed to live out the rest of his life in exile, and Giuseppe rose to the status of don at last.

Once he was the head of all crime in Palermo, Giuseppe did two major things. Firstly, he started to aggressively expand his crime family's organizations. He leveraged his contributions in the Mafia war that had just ended to convince the Corleones to allow him to take territories from smaller, weaker families who had not contributed as much as he had during the war. Upon his annexation of several surrounding territories, the Greco crime family's turf rivaled that of the Corleones themselves. This created tension between the two families, especially when Giuseppe stopped listening to the Corleones as he once had.

The second major thing that Giuseppe did when he became don was to expand his organization to create a wing dedicated solely to contract killing. He offered his services to rival crime families, assembling a team of over fifty contract killers, all of whom he personally vetted in order to ensure that they would be up to the difficult task of conducting kills all across the country.

The various crime families that Giuseppe lent his services to were more than happy to hand over their dirty work to someone else. Even the Corleones ended up hiring Giuseppe and his band of killers to conduct hits. The political game that Giuseppe played here was utterly brilliant. He made each crime family think that he was loyal to them and no one else, when in fact he was often responsible for killing members of the two rival families, working simultaneously for each organization. This move was brilliant for two reasons.

Firstly, it created tension amongst a lot of families which weakened their position a great deal and made them sloppy when it came to their criminal activities. Secondly, it made him an important person in other criminal families as well. He was not just the don of his own Mafia family, he was respected and welcome in the homes of pretty much every other don in the country. This meant that he was the only person that was not on the brink of war with some other crime family.

This was all done in an attempt to create so much dissent that another war would begin, except this time he would turn it into a war against the Corleones. Before the Mafia war, there were several ruling families, all of which had smaller families that they provided territory to. However, when the Corleones emerged victorious in the war, they became the dictators of the Cosa Nostra, monopolizing every aspect of the criminal underworld in Sicily. Many crime families resented this, and Greco was primed to use this to his advantage.

The Corleones were not considered one of the greatest families in the history of the Cosa Nostra for no reason. They managed to quell the unrest that was brewing and, as a result, Giuseppe ended up losing a lot of the territory he had gained since the Corleones decided that spreading his territory around a bit would make the other families more accepting of their dictatorship. This ploy worked, and it left Giuseppe with far less profits than he had once commanded.

Renewed Focus on Contract Killing

Now that Giuseppe did not have drugs and the like to worry about, he was able to focus on the one branch of his organization that was still left standing:

the contract killers. This also played into his need for vengeance, because he wanted to pay back the Corleones, along with a lot of other families, for taking away everything he had worked so hard to gain.

Even though Giuseppe was no longer respected as a Mafiosi, he was still considered a highly skilled contract killer, and his force of killers was frequently hired by the various criminal outfits to conduct hits. He began to raise his rates and provide kills that were unheard of, such as the murders of small-time politicians and other prominent members of society. This gave him a small amount of power, nothing close to what he had once had, but still enough that he was able to maintain the influence that he had over the younger Mafiosi in pretty much every crime family in the country.

The End of the His Career

Because Giuseppe had become a bit of a nuisance, the other Mafia families started plotting his demise. Once he lost everything, Greco had started to cause a lot of problems and raise a lot of ruckus, and this had made it difficult for families to continue to do business in their territories. Greco was definitely the sort of man that had a revolutionary mind, and this mind had ideas that made the other crime families very uncomfortable indeed. Hence, they were more than willing to have him killed.

The truly sad part about Giuseppe's end is that he was killed not by his enemies but by his friends.

While the younger Mafiosi idolized him, his contemporaries, even those that were in the same family as him, felt like he was too much of a maverick to allow him to continue disrupting their operations. Hence, two of his friends ended up tricking him into coming over to their home and shot him dead.

He was found by authorities who recognized him immediately as one of the most wanted men in Sicily, and they decided to take him in and conduct an autopsy. Now that they had his body, they were free to conduct an investigation, and a trial was conducted. During this trial, Greco was posthumously sentenced to life in prison. He was proven guilty of fifty-eight murders, although his long and illustrious career meant that he might very well have murdered far more people than this.

Meanwhile, Greco's friends and murderers were trying to handle the aftermath of what they had done. Giuseppe had been so popular among the youth that he had started to become seen as a martyr, and this was causing a lot of unrest among the Mafia clans. In order to erase him from memory completely, the various Mafia clans stole his body from the morgue and destroyed it. Greco's corpse was immersed in acid until there was nothing left of him. This meant that Giuseppe had no grave that people could come to and remember him. He now existed only as an idea in the minds of the younger Mafiosi, and the dons of the time were able to quell these ideas without much difficulty now that Greco was no more.

Blood Money: The Method and Madness of Assassins

All in all, Greco died as one of the most successful contract killers ever to walk the earth. By some estimates, he was considered to be directly responsible for hundreds of murders, and if you take into account the murders conducted by the various men he had under his employ, the number could be far higher than that, too. Greco remains an iconic figure in the criminal underworld, and even though the younger Mafiosi never ended up truly revolting, Greco's ideas still influenced their decisions once they achieved higher ranks in the criminal underworld. His influence can still be seen today, as the Cosa Nostra has become a lot more democratic, although Greco might not have approved that much of the lack of violence in modern day Sicily.

Glennon Engleman – The Dentist

There is nothing quite as intriguing as a contract killer that lives a double life, especially when the double life ends up being rather mundane. Glennon Engleman worked as a dentist and a fairly successful one at that, but he also worked as a contract killer. He is one of the more unique contract killers in this list because he had a different approach to his kills entirely. Instead of being part of some kind of criminal organization, Engleman killed for people that just wanted revenge. His most common hires were made by people that were seeking insurance claims. As you already know, life insurance claims are perhaps the most popular uses for contract killers. Engleman exemplified this fact. In spite of his long and fairly successful career as a contract killer, Engleman never took part in any other criminal activities.

Early Life

One of the many things that sets Engleman apart from the contract killers mentioned before, along with the general stereotype that surrounds contract killers in general, is the fact that he was not raised in an abusive home. In fact, his childhood was actually quite pleasant, all things considered. He was the youngest of four children, all of whom were born and raised in Missouri. His father was a member of the United States Air Force, and while this made him quite strict about a variety of things, he was not abusive in any way.

Engleman's early life was the epitome of middle class, Midwestern Americana. He lived in a nice house that his parents owned, he had a lawn where he shared mowing duties with his brothers, and he did fairly well in school, although he never really excelled in any particular subject. Yet, there was one aspect to Engleman's personality that most people in his life simply did not recognize: the fact that he was a sociopath.

A sociopath is essentially someone that does

not feel any kind of empathy or remorse. They fail to see why other people cannot be harmed, and this is what leads to a lot of sociopaths becoming manipulative and abusive, at the very least, and extremely violent murderers in worst case scenarios. Over the course of his life, Engleman proved time and time again that his was a worst case scenario.

His sociopathic nature was not the result of his upbringing. Such psychological conditions are often the result of genetic abnormalities, although Engleman's family did not have a history of this condition. Even though he did not feel any empathy nor did he feel strong emotions in any way, Engleman learned early on how to put on a mask and fake it. This is one of the biggest reasons why he was able to lie low even though he worked as a contract killer for an extended period of time.

He did not display any outwardly violent tendencies, but he was responsible for the deaths of various animals to which he ended up confessing after his eventual capture and incarceration. He described how he would capture his neighbor's pets, torture them for hours and then kill them. When asked why he did this, Engleman said that he was simply curious. According to him, he just wanted to know what would happen. This is highly common behavior among sociopaths, and it is theorized that they do this in an attempt to feel something, since they realize early on that most other people have something that they do not.

A Mediocre, Boring Life

Engleman did not start killing until much later on in his life. His teens passed without a single kill, at least as far as humans are concerned, and Engleman graduated from Washington University in St. Louis, Missouri, as a dentist after which he immediately began to practice. His patients frequently complained to his superiors that Engleman had a very odd bedside manner. He was not creepy per se, but there were just certain things about him that were odd. After Engleman was sentenced to life in prison when he was arrested and convicted, many people came forward to describe how he seemed to have absolutely no emotion in his eyes. Whenever he would laugh or talk to somebody at all, his eyes would remain emotionless and dead. This is because Engleman was pretty much faking it the whole time. He just did not have the skills to change the way his eyes moved, as this is the sort of thing that only experienced actors can accomplish.

Unusual Beginnings

At the age of 31, after having practiced dentistry for five years and setting up his own practice, Engleman started seeing a woman that would become his first wife. This woman was named Edna Ruth, and the problem with their relationship was that she was already married. Ruth frequently complained about her husband and told Engleman that she was not happy with him at all. She was one of the few people that were able to recognize the fact that Engleman was a sociopath quite early on, and she decided to use this knowledge to her advantage. She suggested to Engleman that there was a way that they could be together and significantly improve their standard of living as well. Her husband had a lucrative life insurance policy, and if he were to die, Ruth would be able to cash in on said policy. Engleman was more than happy to help; indeed he did not quite understand why this was such a difficult thing to do.

Over the next few days, Engleman bought a gun illegally and used it to kill Ruth's husband. The life insurance policy provided Ruth with over sixty thousand dollars which she used to allow her and Engleman to settle down and buy a house. They soon married which certainly raised a few eyebrows since people found it odd that Ruth would be so willing to settle down with someone mere months after her husband had died. Although this did not cause any problems at that particular moment in time, it did end up factoring into Engleman's downfall decades later.

A Long Career

Engleman had experienced great pleasure in the murder of Ruth's husband, and he decided that he would continue to do things like this. Since he liked the idea of earning money for doing something that he enjoyed, he decided to become a professional contract killer. He accumulated contacts that needed his services over a period of time, and with these contacts, he was eager to use his skills in order to get the same benefits that Engleman and Ruth had gotten after killing Ruth's husband.

Hence, Engleman started to kill people so that their spouses or relatives could cash in on their life insurance claims, and he took a portion of the insurance settlement after the job was successfully completed. As far as modus operandi is concerned, Engleman was pretty much all over the place. He did not have a preferred weapon, using whatever he felt would work best in the particular situation. He often used guns, but he was also known to kill victims using heavy blunt objects such as hammers or even things that were lying around in the general area where he found his victim. Strangulation was another technique that Engleman often employed.

The thing about his modus operandi that remained consistent was his meticulousness. When Engleman received a contract, he would spend weeks stalking his victims and seeing their every move. This allowed him to plan out his kill based on his victim's schedule. He would target his victims in moments where he knew they would be vulnerable and would not be able to call out for help. Once he had killed his victim using whatever technique he was fancying at that moment in time, he would dispose of the remains impeccably, leaving absolutely no trace of foul play. Although all of his confirmed victims' bodies were discovered, he never left any evidence that the police would have been able to use to tie the murders to him, even if they managed to discover proof of foul play through some miracle.

Thanks to his enormous attention to detail, Engleman was able to enjoy a career that lasted thirty years. Most contract killers are lucky if they get to a single decade, but Engleman proved that he was a cut above the rest by lasting thrice that amount of time. One thing that made him so difficult to pin as a contract killer was the fact that he had such an unassuming appearance. If you were to see him walking down the street, you would have assumed that he was just some shy, quiet man that was going about his business. The rotund figure, spectacles, neat side parting and bland button-up shirts that he always wore further increased his invisibility. Simply put, Engleman was the last person that you would notice in a crowd, thus allowing him to avoid any repercussions from authorities for an extended period of time.

Turmoil in Personal Life and Eventual Capture

Even though Engleman is arguably one of the most meticulous contract killers in the history of the occupation, he was not invincible. It is extremely unlikely that a contract killer would be able to go their entire life without getting captured since they were involved in activities that resulted in the deaths of a lot of people. Individuals that hire contract killers often get a guilty conscience, patterns are often found that prove that foul play is coming from a single source, and apart from all this, doing the same thing for thirty years is going to make even the most capable of contract killers complacent. Additionally, emotional instability brought about by turmoil in one's personal life can also contribute to one's downfall.

In Engleman's case, the last possible reason played the most important role in his capture. After being married to Edna Ruth for nearly twenty years, his wife ended up divorcing him. She knew about his career as a contract killer and, after spending so long with him, she was simply unable to come to terms with the fact that her husband was a killer, especially when she realized how much he enjoyed his job. After she left him, Engleman slumped into a deep depression that resulted in him losing a lot of the efficiency that he had once had. Although he married again rather quickly and his next wife bore him a son, Engleman never really recovered because Ruth had been the only person to see the real him and accept him for what he was.

The final decade of his career was marked by some minor sloppiness, but the true mistake occurred when he was hired by the heir to an oil fortune to kill her father so that she could collect a multi-million-dollar life insurance policy and gain access to her father's fortune as well. Although he was successful in this kill and his wealth increased significantly, the person that had hired him ended up getting captured. This contract ended up causing two problems for Engleman

First of all, his client, when arrested, confessed that she had hired a contract killer to do a job for her. While she did not say his name, leaving him more or less safe from any potential legal ramifications, the fact that she had told the police about a contract killer made them connect the dots. Soon, the police in this area realized that a lot of murders they had seen over the past couple of decades had been done by the same contract killer, since they traced Engleman's modus operandi and saw it popping up again and again. Although they did not know that Engleman was the killer, the fact that they had started an investigation meant that there was a chance that they might trace these murders back to him.

Additionally, the sudden influx of a great deal of money turned out to be a problem. Suddenly spending enormous amounts of money that have no legal record can be a problem because the IRS notices things like this and can launch an investigation. Engleman did not take this into account, and he ended up spending a lot of money that he could not attribute to his successful but still small dental practice. Hence, there was now something that could connect him to the murders. He had received a large amount of money at the same time that his previous client's father had been killed. It was now inevitable that the police would end up making the connection.

Although the investigation took a decade to finally complete, during which time Engleman continued his career as a contract killer, in the year 1987 he was finally arrested and charged with four murders that could be directly linked to him. He was sentenced to two life sentences in prison, and during this life sentence, he confessed to the most lucrative contract of his career, the one that was essentially the beginning of his end, making the total number of people that he definitely killed to seven. It is unknown how many people he killed in total that he did not mention, but the number could be far higher than the four he was convicted for and the three he confessed to.

After twelve years of incarceration, Engleman died of natural causes in the year 1999. He is a great example of how contract killers could be the people you least expect, people that you might have thought of as stand-up individuals who would never hurt a fly.

Benjamin Siegel – Bugsy

During the rise of organized crime in America during the first two decades of the twentieth century, there were two main ethnic groups that were known to control a heavy portion of the criminal activities that were going on in places like New York City. One group were the Italians, certainly the most well-known criminals in the world, but another group that a lot of people seem to forget about consists of Jewish Americans. Jewish immigrants in America were usually really poor, so they turned to crime in order to support themselves.

One of the most prolific contract killers hired by the Jewish Mafia was Benjamin Siegel. He was a classic gangster, the sort of person that you watch movies about. Throughout his career he was involved in a number of different criminal activities, all of which ended up playing an important role in him becoming an important figure whenever American crime was discussed.

Early Life

Born in 1908, Siegel grew up in immense squalor that left him thoroughly dissatisfied with his life. New York City is well known for its income disparity, and often poor people like Siegel would catch a glimpse of individuals far richer than they could ever hope to be living glamorous lives that were a far cry from the misery that they had to suffer through. Very early on, Siegel decided that he would not let his circumstances prevent him from doing great things. He wanted it all and he wanted it in the shortest amount of time possible, which is why he did not complete his schooling. Instead, he left school to join a street gang during his mid-teens.

His early years as a criminal were rather innocuous. Essentially he robbed easy targets such as stores in his area using the help of his fellow gang members, but after a few years, he met someone that would change his life. This individual was Moe Sedway, and he ended up becoming the person that helped Siegel branch out into a wider world of crime that would become far more profitable for him in the future.

Beginning of Criminal Career

With his new partner, Siegel ended up starting the most basic and yet profitable enterprise that a reasonably organized criminal outfit could attempt: a protection racket. Hapless business owners would be coerced into paying Siegel and Sedway lest these hoodlums ended up wreaking havoc in their shops.

His early start meant that Siegel was one of the first Jewish Americans to get involved in organized crime, and pretty soon he was recruited by an Italian mob boss which was rather common in those days. This was the era of prohibition, and his boss made an enormous amount of profit selling illegal alcohol to people that needed it. The Italian don wanted to expand his operations and start selling to Jewish neighborhoods, but he knew that if he had a Jewish face to represent his dealings in these areas, it would be far more likely that he would secure regular buyers.

Thus, Siegel, Sedway and a third man that had become their partner named Meyer Lansky ended up coming together to start this bootlegging racket, thanks to the help of their Mafioso friend. This trio of criminals decided to provide services to as many people as possible in order to ensure that they would not have to worry about being restricted to a single source of income.

Siegel went one step further by starting a career as a hit man. He noticed that the Italian boss he worked for, as well as certain Irish mobsters and those within the Jewish community, had enemies that they needed to have taken care of. Siegel, being an enterprising individual who always knew how to take advantage of an opportunity, offered to help these criminal bosses by killing their enemies for them.

Over the next few years, Siegel and his partners branched out into drugs as well, and Siegel continued to work as a contract killer on the side. He used his contracts to kill people for money, and he also stole their drugs or alcohol from them, thus allowing him to increase profits on both ends of his criminal enterprise. Pretty soon, Siegel was earning enough money to afford a lot of the luxury he had once dreamed of, but he was not quite done. Siegel was not the sort of person that was easily satisfied.

Rise of Organized Crime

As his operations started to grow, Siegel began to make a lot of contacts in the criminal underworld. One was an individual by the name of Charles "Lucky" Luciano, someone that would play an important role in both Siegel's future as well as the future of organized crime in general.

When the 1930s began, organized crime was really chaotic and poorly managed. Small gangs were fighting one another for territory, and the larger criminal syndicates were using their power to muscle smaller families out of their territories, which left a lot of violent people unemployed, thus leading to violence which in turn lead to an even bigger increase in police activity.

Luciano was a very forward-thinking person. He was a powerful criminal and he had a lot of respect among the various crime families that existed across America. As a result he had a voice that people would usually listen to. Siegel's partner, Lansky, wanted to unite the Italian and Jewish criminal traditions into a single entity, a sort of governing body that would bring a semblance of order to crime in America. Lansky provided the idea, Luciano had the influence, and together they created an elite council of dons that distributed territory fairly so that everyone would have a piece of the pie. The goal of this was to prevent excess violence which had been resulting in disastrous police crackdowns.

In the wake of this new criminal order, Siegel created his own crime family which he called Murder, Incorporated. Involved in everything from drugs to bootlegging to prostitution, Siegel's new crime syndicate was pretty much as successful as an outfit like this could possibly get, but he was unhappy. He had experienced a lot of success and had gained a lot of wealth, but one of the biggest draws that the criminal world had for Siegel was the fact that it was chaotic. There were not supposed to be any rules, and Siegel chafed at the impositions being imposed on him by men that he considered his equals.

He left his own syndicate and became a contract killer exclusively. He also set his sights westward to California where he knew there was the potential to earn a lot of money from the rules that Luciano and Lansky were trying to enforce. After several years of killing criminals for money, Siegel had ended up making a great many enemies that wanted him dead. Left with no place to hide, he decided that it was time to move to California.

In Los Angeles, Siegel made a lot of contacts and ended up earning ten times the money he had been earning on the east coast. This success was short lived, however, as Siegel was ousted by a hostile takeover initiated by a Chicago-based crime family. By this point, he had already made a lot of investments, and he had a thriving prostitution ring as well. In addition to this, he had made a lot of friends in high places, so he was ready to move on to the next stage of his life, even though he was greatly incensed by how he had been ousted from something he had built through hard work.

He moved to Las Vegas where he tried to start a new life that was free from crime. He purchased a casino that was extremely extravagant, one of the first signs that Las Vegas was to become an exceedingly popular destination for gambling in the future. He earned enormous amounts of money here, and he used it to finance an incredibly luxurious lifestyle full of excess.

Downfall

Even though he had killed so many people during his career as a hit man, murder was not what Siegel ended up being arrested for. It was tax evasion, something that brought down a good friend of Siegel's who became an iconic figure in American crime, a man by the name of Al Capone.

Siegel had a lot of undeclared income, and soon he had federal authorities on his back. Once he was arrested, he began to build a case for himself. A career full of enormous projects begun but never truly finished seemed destined to provide nothing but failure for Siegel, and in this case, he was once again unable to finish what he started.

His enemies were able to get to him at last because he no longer had access to the small army of private guards that he used to take with him everywhere. Hence, in this vulnerable state, Siegel ended up getting killed. A contract killer getting killed by another contract killer, Siegel's end was almost poetic in a way.

It is also theorized that Siegel's death was caused by his arrest, revealing that he had been stealing money from the various criminal organizations he had been working with for several years. Hence, there is a good chance that his death was retribution for his various misdeeds.

Blood Money: The Method and Madness of Assassins

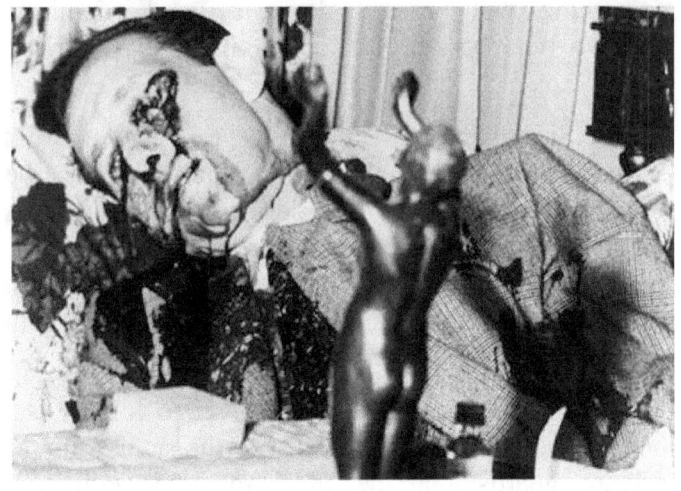

Siegel's career may not be as successful as that of previously mentioned contract killers in this book, but it is important to note that he was instrumental in the rise of organized crime in its modern form, and without his contributions, the future prevalence of contract killers and their association with organized crime would never have come about. Hence, Siegel is a highly iconic contract killer, and much like Vincent Coll did for the Irish mob, Siegel gave a lot of inspiration to the future generations of Jewish professional criminals. He and Coll are arguably the inventors of contract killing in its modern form, and Siegel managed to prove his superiority to Coll by enjoying a far longer and far more successful career where he branched out into a variety of different criminal enterprises, all of which earned him enormous amounts of money. It can be argued that his childhood dream actually did come true.

Female Assassins that Took the World by Storm

One of the biggest stereotypes associated with assassins and contract killers is the concept that they are all men. This is not true at all. Some of the most successful and prolific contract killers in history have been women. These assassins made a mark on the world because they always took their victims by surprise. A man generally would not perceive a woman to be a threat, and these women used this underestimation to their advantage!

Mata Hari

One of the biggest mistakes that men make is that they tend to objectify women so much that it becomes impossible for them to see the legitimate threat that these women might pose. Mata Hari is a great example of how a female assassin used this objectification to hide in plain sight. Her real name was Margaretha MacLeod, and she was born in the Netherlands. She soon started to work as a dancer, performing exotic dances for high-ranking officials all across Europe.

She was in great demand, but what the officials that hired her did not know was that she was secretly a German spy, or rather a contract killer hired by German intelligence to kill people on their behalf. She accomplished her tasks by offering private dances to multiple people, one of whom was the person she intended to kill. Once the dances were over and Mata Hari had left, the dead body of her victim would be found and she would be long gone.

The true brilliance of her technique was that she appeared so meek and unassuming, so submissive, that the men investigating these deaths never thought to suspect her, even though there was a clear pattern to be seen.

The career of a contract killer is destined to be a short lived one, and this was true for Mata Hari as well. After passing on vast amounts of intelligence to Germany and taking out key figures in the Allied camps, she was captured by a British spy and sentenced to death. She only managed to stay active for three years, but during these three years, she accomplished things that other contract killers would not have come close to in an entire decade. Hence, Mata Hari played an important role in shaping the world and proving that women can be deadly contract killers too.

Kim Hyun-Hui

This North Korean woman was the sort of person that most people would not even look at twice if they ever saw her on the street. This was part of what made her such an effective killer. She worked for the North Korean government, carrying out contract killings on their behalf. Her tasks included destabilizing rebel movements by killing their leaders and killing political opponents at the whim of the labyrinthine system of government that exists in

Pyongyang.

She was thoroughly trained before being sent on her missions, and as a result, she had the skills necessary to successfully kill her targets. One unique aspect of her modus operandi is the fact that she preferred using bombs rather than other weapons. This is because she was usually tasked with killing multiple people unlike most contract killers who are generally only given a single target.

Once she was captured, she ended up defecting to South Korea since she had no other option. Her current location is unknown, but it is known that she is married and has a child now. Her curse is one that many contract killers have to deal with. She was responsible for attacks on South Korean soil, so she will never be accepted as a true citizen of that country. Additionally, she betrayed the country of her birth, and so she can never go back to North Korea either and has to constantly fear North Korea trying to capture her in order to punish her for what she did.

Contract killers have to deal with the fact that they are the ones that have to deal with both sides. In the end, both sides often end up rejecting them. This is perhaps the reason that contract killers are often loners; it is certainly the case with Hyun-Hui.

Brigitte Mohnhaupt

Although not a contract killer in the classical sense, Mohnhaupt was still a very prolific assassin who mostly killed for political reasons above all others. This is because she was a member of a radical left wing group. The purpose of this group was to spread communism by any means necessary, and Mohnhaupt played her part by killing people that she considered capitalists who contributed to the oppression of the working class.

Throughout her career, she killed dozens of people and used a variety of different techniques to do it. Although she was never paid for her work, it can be argued that the fact that she was furthering her group's political agenda served as payment enough for her. Whatever the case may be regarding how she was paid, the fact of the matter remains that Mohnhaupt was frequently recruited to carry out attacks on people that were against this group and all that it stood for.

Maria Jimenez

In a mostly male-dominated criminal underworld, Jimenez managed to make a name for herself by being far more brutal than any man that participated in contract killing. Over the course of her brief but violent career, she was involved in drug trafficking and killed almost two dozen people for money.

Mexico is a land generally known for its machismo, so the fact that Jimenez was able to make such a huge mark on the country is a very impressive feat. She was frequently assigned to kill men far heavier and stronger than she was, but her enormous skills as an assassin allowed her to take her victims down with ease. A superior hand-to-hand combatant as well as an expert marksman, Jimenez had all of the makings of a successful career before she was arrested and convicted.

Contract Killers in Fiction

Because of the intriguing and mysterious nature of contract killers, a lot of movies have used this archetype for its characterizations. These characters vary wildly in their depictions, with some being portrayed as dangerous criminals while others are treated in a very sympathetic and often humorous manner. There are a few depictions of contract killers that truly stand out because they impacted the way the general public views this profession, and even had an impact on how contract killers were perceived in the criminal underworld to a lesser extent.

Vincent in Collateral

Tom Cruise is highly respected superstar who has played a wide variety of characters. One of his most underrated performances is in the film "Collateral" where he portrays a hit man that has been contracted to kill witnesses that might testify against a drug kingpin. He takes a cab driver hostage and makes him drive him to the various locations where his victims are.

This is definitely one of the more nuanced portrayals of a contract killer seen in film. The character of Vincent is defined by shades of grey. He is a brutal killer, but he does not find pleasure in killing, nor does he inflict violence when it is not necessary. At the end of the film when the cab driver, played by Jamie Foxx, shoots Vincent in the stomach, Vincent is surprised but does not hold it against Jamie

Foxx's character, thereby portraying this contract killer as someone that accepts the consequences of the job he chose.

Tom Cruise's performance in this movie manages to gain the audience's sympathy in spite of how violent he is, and humanizes these individuals in a way. One can say that it is not a very accurate portrayal since it romanticizes the concept quite a bit.

Agent 47 in Hitman

Hitman was a highly popular video game that spawned a series of games, all of which have garnered significant acclaim. As you can probably tell from the title, the main character is a hit man named Agent 47, and your primary objective is to kill people you have been contracted to kill. The portrayal of a contract killer in this game is quite fantastical, since the protagonist is a genetically engineered clone that has been designed to be a killing machine.

Additionally, the character is portrayed in a rather sympathetic light in spite of his violence and cold-bloodedness. His tragic backstory allows the audience to empathize with him and enables people to view him as the hero even though he kills people for money. Over the course of the game, Agent 47 starts to change his outlook on life and realizes that he does not have to kill. The empathy he learns over the course of the game attempts to give the character a fresh start and allow him to become a legitimate hero that the player can root for.

This character is important because it

indicates how the life of a contract killer is glorified and can be exploited to provide people with escapist entertainment.

Lorne Malvo in Fargo

Fargo was originally a film that portrayed a man that hires a hit man to kill his wife for him. The television version of the film tells a similar story, with a hit man named Lorne Malvo playing a central role. Malvo is a ruthless, cold, but inherently calm figure who has no qualms whatsoever about violence. While he doesn't seem to enjoy violence in particular, he does like knowing that people are afraid of him and uses his skills as a killer to frequently intimidate the people around him.

The contract killer in this show seems to be some kind of freelancer rather than a hired gun. He is apparently so in demand that he travels across the country, and while this is not exactly common, it has been the way that a lot of contract killers have operated before. One thing that stands out about this character is the fact that he always seems to know what to do in order to get out of a tight situation.

A Common Thread

One thing that most of the serious portrayals of contract killers have in common is that they portray these killers as some kind of superhuman that can get out of pretty much any situation they find themselves in. They are portrayed as extremely physically strong, master marksmen, and borderline geniuses as well who can outsmart everyone around them and get rid of the evidence in such a way that no one would be able to find them.

This is obviously not a very accurate portrayal. Contract killers were usually just thugs who were hired by organized crime to do things for them so that they would not have to worry about the legal ramifications. Real contract killers were not evil geniuses that had three backup plans in case Plan A failed. Often they did not have a plan at all; they just waited until they found their moment and took it while hoping for the best.

There have been some contract killers who had entire movies made about them. One of the most prominent examples is Richard Kuklinski. The movie about Kuklinski suffered the same problems that most Hollywood movies face. They glossed over the darker aspects of his personality and only went for the sort of violence that would entice a crowd. This erased a lot of the evil that Kuklinski committed, although they certainly did not portray him in a sympathetic light. But, they did portray him as a criminal mastermind who was always a step ahead. While it is true that Kuklinski was smart, at the end of the day, he was a brute as well who loved to kill for pleasure. Movies, films and games that depict contract killers generally overestimate their abilities and paint them to be super-soldiers, when in reality they are just criminals with guns and are often no more capable at handling the job than you would be.

Joseph Sullivan – The Mad Dog

Once again we are about to delve into the world of organized crime, a world that time and time again has proved to be a true breeding ground for contract killers, a place where they could hone their skills and acquire a steady source of income. In this chapter, we are going to discuss Joseph Sullivan, a contract killer who was referred to as Mad Dog for his brutal, uninhibited nature which obviously leaked into his killings, making him one of the most vicious contract killers in this entire list.

Early Life

By this point you have probably realized that the contract killers on this list are often united by the fact that their childhoods were not the most fulfilling experiences for them. In fact, their childhoods often left them with the sort of trauma that would cause them to eventually turn to a life of crime!

This is certainly the case with Joseph Sullivan. In his case, during the earliest years of his childhood, he actually had a pretty good life. His parents were supportive, particularly his father, who served as a great role model for Sullivan and was the epitome of a hard-working, blue collar individual. His life with his family in Queens was far from idyllic, but at the same time, it is important to note the fact that he was still quite happy because the lack of money was not the sort of thing that could take happiness away from such a close-knit family.

At the age of thirteen, Sullivan was on the cusp of becoming a man, and it was at this age that he truly needed his father to provide him with guidance and support. This was the age when his father died. The trauma of his father's passing shook Sullivan and made him retreat inward. He stopped talking for some time, and in addition to this, he started to develop a slightly aggressive streak.

The latter was actually in response to his mother's abuse. Following the death of her husband, Sullivan's mother began to be quite abusive to her son. This was partly because Sullivan was the spitting image of his father, and she hated the fact that her son had now become a reminder of what she had lost. In her grief, she became a very toxic influence in her son's life, one that gave him a great deal of anger issues that he never really got over.

In order to overcome his anger issues and release some of the frustration that tended to build up because he was so thoroughly unloved, he started picking fights at school. This was only the tip of the iceberg, though. In no time at all, Sullivan was going to display much more extreme levels of violence, the sort of thing that would lead to him becoming one of the most brutal killers in the history of contract killing.

A Transient Existence

After Sullivan's father died, his relatives attempted to give him a home with them since they had noticed how abusive his mother was. This should have been an ideal arrangement, but for some reason, Sullivan could just not wrap his head around the fact that these people he barely even knew were the now the people responsible for taking care of him.

He ran away from their home and returned to his mother, hoping that he could get some semblance of his old life back. The loss of both her husband and her son had turned Sullivan's mother into a heavy drinker, and her alcoholism made her thoroughly unfit to take care of her son.

At the age of fourteen, over a year after his father had died, Sullivan ended up running away from home permanently. He made his way initially as a pickpocket, but soon he had to resort to some more creative measures such as breaking and entering. He was never caught while committing any of these crimes, but it is important to note that he was arrested in a way for vagrancy.

Because he was caught on the streets, he ended up getting sent to a reformatory school. For the next five years, he was in and out of reformatory schools, trying to escape every time, only to be caught yet again and taken back. He was left with an extremely fractured childhood because he never really had a home after the age of thirteen, and this made him very isolated. Additionally, these reformatory schools were very tough places where he had to fight to survive with the other violent children.

Sullivan was nineteen when he finally escaped reformatory schools for good, and he decided to join the army in order to have a place where he could finally belong. It was in the army that he learned the various skills he needed in order to become the best contract killer possible.

Post Army Life

During his army days, he learned how to kill with the most efficiency possible, which certainly struck a chord with his violent side, but at the same time, he was not able to follow the strict rules that pretty much everyone in the army simply had to follow.

Hence, his penchant for running away ended

up making him leave the army as well, at which point he was left with no option but to go into hiding. He committed several crimes during this period of hiding, and finally ended up killing his first man. This led to his very first arrest, landing him with a prison sentence in Attica for manslaughter.

Much like the other contract killers that are on this list, Sullivan made the contacts necessary for him to excel in his career as a contract criminal while he was in prison. It was also in prison that he got the nickname Mad Dog, partly because he was so brutal and violent and partly because he had a disorder of his salivary gland that made him drool a lot.

Mad Dog gained a great deal of notoriety in prison for two big reasons. First of all, he was able to gain notoriety for his violence and his willingness to fight for people that he was loyal to, as well as the fact that he ended up escaping from a prison that was thought to be impossible to escape from.

This made him a celebrity in the criminal underworld, and Mad Dog had a lot of contacts waiting for him on the outside. He ended up working for a crime family that was extremely influential, and they were able to provide him with the necessary tools to stay safe. Although he was arrested and sent back to prison, his new employers hired a lawyer for him that was able to get him parole in no time at all, something that was pretty remarkable when you take into account the fact that he had already escaped from prison and thoroughly deserved to be in jail for a much longer period of time.

Once he had acquired his freedom, Mad Dog started to make a name for himself as a contract killer. All his life he had been searching for a place where he would not be an outsider, a place where he would be considered a part of the family. Now that he was a part of this family, he felt that at last. Everyone in the crime family respected him, and some even feared him. Mad Dog certainly enjoyed that because it made him feel powerful, something that he certainly did not mind feeling on a regular basis.

The thing about Mad Dog was that he was dedicated to his work. He was the sort of person that liked to both work hard and play hard. He worked for fourteen hours a day, tirelessly attempting to gather as much information about the people he was going to kill as possible. He was also made one of the most important people in the drug trade, so he had to handle that. However, after he completed his work day, he did not just go home and sleep. Instead, he spent the riches he was earning as one of the most in demand contract killers in the country to create a name for himself as a hard partier too.

He barely slept for several years, using cocaine to keep himself awake and only going to sleep when his body truly couldn't take any more of the abuse he was giving it. This was one of the reasons why Mad Dog is such an intriguing figure. While a lot of the contract killers on this list have been known for being cold and uncaring, Mad Dog was the exact opposite of this. Where other contract killers were hollow and cold, Mad Dog was always full of life. He spent his money freely and relished the idea of having friends, which is in stark contrast to the other contract killers in this list who seemed to avoid relationships like the plague.

It is rather intriguing that the reason that most contract killers avoid friendships did not come into play in Mad Dog's career. He was never betrayed, he never got sloppy because he was involved in other people's lives. Sullivan was responsible for his own demise, so perhaps the theory that contract killers need to be dead on the inside in order to do what they do is not all that accurate. It certainly wasn't accurate in the case of Mad Dog Sullivan.

A Brief, Ascendant Career

Sullivan soared to the top and stayed there for the next six years. He married and had two children, and one of his loved ones was able to figure out that he was one of the most feared individuals in the criminal underworld. This fact made it absolutely impossible for them to understand what was in store for the future, and Sullivan was certainly not going to tell them that the comfortable life they took for granted could come crashing down on them at pretty much any moment in time.

After a couple of years, Sullivan had created a name for himself as someone that could handle drugs as well from a business point of view, which made him an extremely important member of the mob that he was a part of. Because he was so well thought of in the mob, pretty much everyone that was involved in his crimes felt proud that they were close to such an individual.

One area that Sullivan excelled in the most was killing rival mob bosses. He had a tendency to be absolutely fearless, something that allowed him to get into situations that other contract killers would have thought about ten times before actually getting into them. This meant that he was able to conduct some of the most spectacular kills that had ever been accomplished in the world of contract killing. This only made him even more famous than he already was, spreading his notoriety like wildfire. If there was one thing that had the potential to provide contract killers with value on the market, it was notoriety. Such a thing was utterly beyond compare because it showed prospective clients that there was nothing the killer in question wouldn't do in order to get the job done as quickly as possible.

During the six years he was active, Sullivan managed his three separate lives perfectly. He was the consummate killer, the consummate partier and the consummate husband. His years of drug use ended up making him rather sloppy. He began to make mistakes, and in 1981 he was arrested. By this point it was rumored that Sullivan had killed several dozen men, which made him one of the most prolific killers in recent times.

He was eventually convicted of three murders,

and was given a life sentence for each of them.

Chester Wheeler Campbell
-The 007 of Detroit

One city that has been slightly underrepresented so far is Detroit. It is very important to keep in mind the fact that Detroit is undoubtedly one of the most crime ridden cities in America. Crime conducted there is just a great deal more vicious than it is in other cities because it is a rather lawless town where gangs often don't end up suffering the sort of consequences they would if they were in cities like New York or Los Angeles.

Chester Campbell is widely considered to be one of the most iconic figures in the world of organized crime within Detroit. It is important to note that he was a slightly different sort of contract killer from the other killers that have been mentioned above because his modus operandi extended beyond just his killing sprees. He played a role in the development of an entire crime syndicate, and this is one of the main reasons why he is such a seminal and widely discussed figure in the world of organized crime.

Early Life

Campbell was a Detroit native who was born and bred in one of the more low end, struggling neighborhoods in the city. His father was quite abusive towards him, so Campbell tended to be out of the house quite often. Since he did not have a lot of money, his free time was spent doing things with the people he made friends with in his neighborhood. This was a rough crowd, and they turned Campbell into a hardened criminal rather quickly.

The thing about life in cities such as this is that loyalty means everything. You can't have someone that is disloyal; people are going to cast him out and turn him into a pariah. Hence, when Campbell joined his first gang, he learned that if he stayed loyal, it meant that he would always have a place to belong. In many ways this continued the tradition that you might have already noticed among the aforementioned killers. This trend involves these killers suffering through abusive or neglectful childhoods, joining gangs in order to feel like they belong, and then the combination of a tendency towards violence as well as a desire to be respected among what was essentially an adopted family, resulting in these individuals turning to a life of contract killing.

The life of crime that Campbell embarked on was the end result of a highly directionless existence. It can be argued that was because he also had a sense of responsibility towards his family. His father was notorious for not giving that much importance to the wellbeing of his loved ones, and Campbell was often left to fend for not just himself but for his mother and siblings as well.

Entry into Contract Killing

The reason that Campbell's life has such an air of tragedy around it is because he was thrust rather unwillingly into the world of contract killing. It was mostly financial reasons that he finally decided to take up this job.

By his early twenties, Campbell had already killed his first victim, except this was someone that he killed out of anger rather than for money. During his teenage years, he had created contacts with a number of different gangs as well, and the efficiency with which he had conducted his first kill ended up causing his name to float around as an option for criminal bosses who needed to get someone killed.

The period during which Campbell was active was a highly volatile one for Detroit in general. The city has a long and sordid history of violence and crime, but during Campbell's era, this violence had in many ways reached its peak because the drug trade was up for grabs. The previous kingpins had met their inevitable downfalls, and now everyone was looking for a way to get in on the action. Since Campbell felt a great deal of loyalty towards the people that he was in a gang with, he ended up taking part in the war that was occurring as a contract killer. He was instrumental in killing rival gang leaders as well as prominent soldiers that were inflicting heavy losses to his own gang. By the time the war was over, Campbell's contributions had been so significant that his gang of underdogs now had a seat at the victor's table, which made Campbell a highly important person as well.

Expansion into the Drug Trade

Now that Campbell was a prominent criminal in Detroit, he started to use his influence to ensure that he profited as much as he could on the name that he had now made for himself. By far the most profitable racket that could be invested in was the drug trade, and since Campbell's efforts during the gang wars resulted in his gang's victory, he had the ability to take significant control of the drugs that came into the city.

He streamlined distribution and created an organized network that reduced accountability by a large margin, and by the time he was finished, the drug trade had become a great deal more peaceful.

Yet, at heart Campbell was still a killer. He had been doing it for so long that he did not know how to stop anymore, and so he continued to kill for money much like all of the other aforementioned contract killers who ended up going into the drug trade.

Modus Operandi

One of the most intriguing aspects of Campbell's career was how he conducted his kills. He did not just follow his victims around until they revealed something that he would be able to use in order to successfully kill them. Instead, he had constant surveillance running on people that he felt could be potential targets in the future. This allowed him to stay prepared for whatever the situation might call for. His clients knew that he had the information to conduct pretty much any kill they would ask him for with ease, and this allowed Campbell to charge large amounts of money for his services. Indeed, his charges were so high that it is surprising that criminals in the city were actually willing to pay them. It is a testament to his talent that he managed to get the usually immensely stingy criminal leaders of Detroit to cough up small fortunes for the opportunity to get Campbell to go after someone they wanted dead.

The information that he collected was also very useful at keeping him safe. All of the criminal leaders in the city knew that Campbell had something or the other on them, and so pretty much everybody was afraid of crossing him. Since they knew that

Campbell had an angry streak that he showed time and time again, they were often afraid to haggle with him as well. This is another thing that probably ensured Campbell's enormously high rates. Due to the intelligence that he consistently collected throughout his career, Campbell ended up gaining dirt on a lot of minor politicians in the city as well. He used these politicians to learn a little about his enemies in public office, and the policemen that he had under his thumb told him everything he needed to know in order to prevent his arrest for a very long period of time.

It is important to note that Campbell's dedication to collecting blackmail material on anyone that might have been a potential target for him is indicative of just how utterly intelligent he was. Generally, contract killers are thought of as evil brutes that have absolutely no sophistication whatsoever. While it is certainly true that Campbell was a murderer who had no qualms about taking another human being's life, it is also important to note that he was not unintelligent in the slightest. Rather, he was the sort of person that had the ability to use his street smarts as well as his keen intellect to get the job done in the most efficient way possible.

Personality

Campbell was widely known to be a hard partier. He loved women, and he was famous for being a playboy. It is theorized that a lot of women were attracted to him because he was such an efficient killer. This attracted the sort of woman that liked danger. He was certainly an exciting person to be around, with his frequent drug use making him a prime candidate for women that were looking for a free high. This is probably why Campbell managed to be such a playboy in spite of the fact that he had a real reputation for being extremely abusive, and that most of the women he dated ended up getting hurt in some way.

A big part of why so many women seemed to like him had to do with the fact that Campbell had an extremely charming personality. He was the sort of person that could silence an entire room full of people upon walking in, and his deep voice and dark, mysterious demeanor certainly made him an ominous figure. Not to mention the fact that he was tall and had naturally broad shoulders, so even when he started to get on in years, Campbell managed to maintain a rather imposing physical presence

Diverse Clientele

The fact that Campbell accumulated so much intelligence and information about pretty much every criminal in the city is not the only thing that makes him stand out so much in the history of contract killing. There is also the fact that he worked with some of the most diverse clients possible.

There is a great divide in the world of crime. The urban gangs and the Mafia are often at odds. Both of them look down on one another and in most cases would never work with each other. Campbell was black, so his allegiance was naturally going to lie with the urban gangs that were comprised almost entirely of people of his own race. The Italians were known to be racist and would not have hired a black hit man in the first place, let alone one that worked for urban gangs. Any black gang member that managed to score a contract with the Italians would almost certainly be cast out by his fellow gang members, so nobody even tried to make something like this work.

Nobody except Campbell, of course. His ability to traverse between two polar opposite worlds was one of his many talents. He was able to blend in with all kinds of crowds, and his confident, charismatic air ensured that anyone that worked with him could feel safe in the knowledge that Campbell would always have things covered.

Hence, Campbell worked for all kinds of criminals. From urban gangs to the Italian Mafia, the Russian Mafia and the Irish mob, Campbell's uncanny knack to bridge cultural divides as if it was no big deal was a very impressive feat indeed. What's truly impressive is that, in spite of the fact that he often killed for opposing sides, he never made as many enemies as you might have thought.

Downfall

Campbell was a highly meticulous killer, so it is rather surprising that he was actually caught. The only reason that the police successfully managed to apprehend him was because he was speeding on an empty road and his car crashed. His car had weapons and drugs inside it, so when the police found him, he was taken into custody. He was eventually connected to several of the murders he had committed, and this resulted in him being sentenced to life in prison. It was a surprising end for one of the greatest hit men Detroit had ever seen. Even after going to prison, Campbell used his considerable intellect to continuously try to get himself out of jail, although pretty much all of his attempts remained unsuccessful.

Wayne Perry – Silk

When you generally think of a contract killer, you tend to think of someone that is stealthy and cautious. A contract killer is generally thought of as someone that can kill without making a peep and then escape without the chance of getting caught. Then you have Wayne Perry, a legend in Washington, DC. His street name was Silk for his smooth-talking personality, but when it came to killing, he was without doubt one of the brashest, most fearless and utterly reckless contract killers that the modern criminal world had ever seen.

There are a number of things that set Perry apart from his ilk, and one of the main things was the fact that he was never afraid to take on a contract. This is part of what made him so popular in the criminal underworld. There was no contract too dangerous for Silk to take, no contract that did not pay enough for him to kill the target within no time at all.

It is a miracle that Perry lasted as long as he did. Some say it was dumb luck, others say it was because he was just that good. Whatever the case may be, it is pretty obvious that Perry is one of the most unique contract killers that one can learn about.

Early Life

Perry grew up in a foster home. This type of upbringing results in a rather maladjusted adult because one is unable to form the sort of attachments that might have formed if one had stayed with one's parents. Perry's father was in prison and his mother was a drug addict, so he really had no option but to stay with his foster family. Although he was reasonably well cared for, the fact that he could not live with his family constantly irked him, and he caused a great deal of problems for his foster parents.

He was regularly responsible for fights and the like, with the neighborhood kids frequently claiming that he got angry if he ever started losing in a sport. This was one aspect of his personality that actually didn't survive into adulthood. Although Perry was always known to be extremely passionate when it came to protecting the people that he was in a gang with, he was not known to get angry very quickly. This contrasts sharply when juxtaposed with the brash and grandiose manners in which he committed his killings.

From a very early age, Perry started selling drugs. He was good at ensuring that the money was never stolen, but at the same time, he was often too brash and chased customers away. In spite of the fact that he was not a very good drug dealer, he was still a capable criminal, and so the people in positions of power within his gang decided to give him the opportunity to become a soldier. This was a highly unusual move, because Perry was still quite young at the time. After becoming a soldier, Perry was responsible for keeping an eye on the corners where drugs were being sold. He was very efficient at ensuring that nobody with ill intent came anywhere near the corners he was protecting.

One aspect of his personality during this phase shone through most of all. This was the fact that he always made a show of how he was protecting his corner. Since he was always visible, he made sure that people knew that he was carrying a weapon, something that often got him into trouble but also cemented his reputation as someone that you absolutely did not want to mess with.

Criminal Expansion

Once Perry started getting involved in crime,

it was just a matter of time before he would end up branching out into a variety of other criminal activities as well. If there is one thing that can be said about Perry, it is that he was definitely an extremely hard worker. He robbed banks, hustled on the streets, and often sold drugs on the side, all while protecting his corner.

He really started to come into the limelight when people started noticing how willing he was to kill. Perry was surrounded exclusively by hardened thugs, but at the same time, many of these thugs still could not be quite as vicious as he was. Perry was an utter animal when he wanted to be, and if he set his eyes on a particular target, there was very little that could be done to prevent that person from dying a horribly painful death.

Seeing Perry's readiness to kill, a lot of the criminal leaders in the city started hiring him as a contract killer. This was one of the most pivotal moments of Perry's life because he started to come into his own as a criminal in the best way possible now. This is because he was just that good at killing. He had the sort of talent that allowed him to go far beyond the sort of killing that other similar criminals would attempt, and his clients particularly liked how bold he was while getting the job done.

Modus Operandi

Now that Perry had established himself somewhat as a contract killer, he approached the tasks he was assigned the way a painter would approach a project that had just been commissioned. Perry was known to walk right up to the people that he needed to kill, shoot them and then walk away like nothing had happened at all.

One might think that this would have led to him easily getting captured, but this was not the case at all. Perry created so much panic because of his brazen violence that most of the time people were just not able to register his face before the deed was done. As a result, Perry managed to create a sort of name for himself. If a criminal leader wanted someone killed publicly in order to send a message, Perry was the man for the job.

He was famous for not really having that many allegiances. He worked for whoever paid him the most money. He had a tight-knit group of friends, but he was known for eschewing the traditional gangster rhetoric of joining a gang and treating the people that are with you in the gang as your family. As a result, there were not that many ways that other criminals could get to him. He was just too insulated from the world for any of the tactics that his fellow criminals might have used in order to take him down.

Widespread Influence

Over the course of his career, Perry started to influence areas that weren't even in his city. Even though he was based in DC, he was involved in a notorious takedown of the Kingpins of Harlem. The drug runners in this city were very territorial, and they were not going to give up their territory very easily at all. This was why Perry was brought in. He was the only person that had the sort of talent that would enable him to easily take the Harlem kingpins down.

The reign of these kingpins ended in a bloody shootout. Perry was one of the last men left standing, and he used this to his advantage. He established his dominance and ruled Harlem with an iron fist. During Perry's reign in Harlem, his reputation made it so that no one even thought of trying to take this particular territory over. As a result, even though Harlem saw its highest levels of drug use in a very long time, the level of violence went down. This is simply because everyone was too afraid of Perry to even think about attacking this territory. They knew that doing so would be nothing short of suicide, and it would result in the gang that tried to attack getting wiped out pretty much entirely.

Reputation

The reputation that Perry amassed while he was in his prime was one of the most fearsome and notorious in criminal history. He was one of the most vicious killers in the city, which meant that he had a lot of enemies, and yet he was known to stroll down the street as if he did not have a care in the world. People were so afraid of him that they decided to just let him pass rather than getting into the hassle of starting a fight with him and inevitably ending up on the losing side.

Perry used this fear to his advantage multiple

times. He used it to make the people that he was hired to kill stop running and accept their fate, he used it to coerce rival gang members into giving him their territory, and he even used it to scare the people that hired him and essentially force them into giving him more money.

All in all, there has never been a contract killer that was as widely feared nor as highly respected as Perry in all of Washington, DC. The things he did remain iconic and are an important part of the city's criminal history now.

Harry Strauss – Pittsburgh Phil

You have already read about Benjamin Siegel and the legacy he left behind. His creation of Murder, Incorporated was one of the most important events in the history of contract killing because it created an organizational structure equivalent to what had been created in Russia and Greece by Alexander Solonik, except in this case the organization ended up being much longer lasting and was bigger than Siegel's individual success.

One of the most successful and notorious members of Murder, Incorporated was Harry Strauss. He was a contemporary of Siegel, but it can be argued that he surpassed even this iconic contract killer because he was focused on just this criminal activity, eschewing the inevitable branching out into drugs and prostitution that most contract killers opt into.

Early Life

Harry Strauss was born in Pittsburgh to parents that were quite toxic. His upbringing was very dysfunctional, but it should be noted that his parents were not abusive towards him at all. Rather, they were abusive towards each other, and seeing the two people that were supposed to be his archetype for all future relationships behaving in such a manner with one another made it difficult for Strauss to get the sort of emotional maturity required for him to form any meaningful connections to other people.

From a young age he was not considered to be particularly bright, with most people assuming that he did not have the sort of talent needed to excel in life. He did have a great deal of physical strength, but he used this to his advantage by playing sports. The problem here was that Strauss's stressful and dysfunctional home life meant that he did not have the sort of emotional and empathy skills necessary to function in a team environment. He managed to find success in wrestling and the like, though, where he relished the chance to release his rage on other people in a way that would not get him into trouble.

Strauss just barely managed to pass high school but then opted not to go to college. It was at this point that he left behind his home life and chose to venture off on his own. Neither he nor his parents knew it at this point, but this would be the last time they would ever see each other. Although Strauss would call his parents on occasion, he never actually met them ever again. Either his criminal career or their own personal problems got in the way whenever they tried to organize something. This left Strauss more or less isolated from anyone that might have reined him in, thus leaving him free to follow the criminal career that he was inevitably going to resort to. The fact that he was so isolated also made him more ruthless than he would have been otherwise, thereby allowing him to secure his reputation as one of the most ruthless contract killers that Pittsburgh had ever seen.

Criminal Beginnings

One of the most unique aspects of Strauss's career is the fact that he did not get his contacts in prison the way that so many of his contemporaries did. Strauss ended up forming his contacts on the outside, and this was considerably more difficult

Since he was a loner, he resorted to crimes that would not have required him to socialize with other people or work in a team. These crimes included things like bank robberies and other instances of theft. He gained notoriety for his unnecessary use of force in such situations, even when the people he was robbing were being cooperative with him.

After spending some time as a criminal and getting arrested a few times, Strauss began to socialize a little bit for the first time in several years.

This was not something he did out of his own need for socialization; rather it was a necessity brought about by the fact that he was now a criminal who needed to launder his money lest he leave a paper trail that the police could follow to convict him.

His money launderer ended up suggesting him to Siegel who was intrigued by what Strauss had to offer. Siegel was setting up Murder, Incorporated during this period, and he was looking for people that had the sort of skills necessary in order to become contract killers. It is important to keep in mind that at this point in time, contract killers were not that plentiful and widespread. Vincent Coll and Benjamin Siegel were really the only prominent examples of people earning money from this kind of criminal activity, which meant that people that might have excelled in such a field might not know that such a thing was possible in the first place.

Siegel met with Strauss and offered to take him under his wing. When Strauss told Siegel that he preferred to work alone, Siegel informed him that even though he would be a member of Murder, Incorporated, he would never have to work with a team. In fact, he would probably never meet any of the other members of the organization since this would help preserve the identities of the other hit men in case anyone from their company ended up getting arrested and snitched to reduce possible prison time. All Strauss would have to do was wait for an assignment to be given to him, after which it would be his job to kill his target by any means necessary.

This was the sort of setup that Strauss would have excelled in, so he agreed to join Murder, Incorporated. After a few days, he got his first assignment. He ended up killing his target, a rival mobster, within two days. Highly impressed by Strauss's performance, Siegel started to assign his new team member a lot more kills and was consistently satisfied by his performance.

Modus Operandi and Kill Count

Over his rather long career, Strauss used a variety of different weapons in order to get the job done. One thing that was regularly missing from his kills was any semblance of routine whatsoever. He had no sort of ritual that he would do in order to complete his kill, unlike many future contract killers such as Richard Kuklinski. Instead, Strauss would kill using anything he had at his disposal. He generally never took a weapon to the place where he intended to kill his victim. Instead, he would try to find a weapon from that very spot and use that to accost and kill his victim. This made him extremely versatile and allowed him to do a lot more kills than he would have been able to complete otherwise. It also removed a bit of his legal vulnerability since he could never be caught carrying a weapon while he was on the way to his victim's location.

One problem that this caused was that Strauss did not plan ways to dispose of his victims. Kuklinski and other contract killers used a ritual to ensure that there would be no evidence to lead police to them while they were conducting their investigation. Since Strauss did not put as much effort into forensic countermeasures, he ended up failing to cover his tracks. His long career was in many ways the product of luck, because the police at this time were quite ineffectual and did not have the sort of forensic techniques that they were going to possess in the future.

Whether he was lucky or just that skillful a killer, the fact of the matter was that Strauss worked as a contract killer for almost a decade. During this period, he is confirmed to have killed over a hundred people based on his own confessions, the confessions of people he had worked with, as well as evidence collected after he had been convicted. However, it is highly likely that the number is far higher. In fact, some people theorize that Strauss killed nearly five hundred people over the course of his career since he was so prolific and did not need very long to complete a kill after it had been assigned.

Downfall

Once Siegel left Murder, Incorporated, a lot of the precautions he had put into place pretty much went out the window. The members started to learn each other's names which put them at risk when one of them was arrested. This person ended up giving the police Strauss's name, and he was thus arrested after a decade of contract killing. After a protracted trial during which he tried to plead insanity, Strauss was sentenced to death. In 1941, he was executed via the electric chair. To this day, the number of people he killed has become something of a legend. It is perhaps this fact that makes him such a pervasive figure in the world of contract killing, with many modern day killers emulating his techniques.

Conclusion

The history of Assassins was inevitable when you consider our society. Criminal entities have always tried to get ahead using illegal means, and in order to meet their goals, they were frequently required to hire the services of someone that was good at killing.

This is probably why contract killing is still alive to this day. One can argue that it is the world's oldest profession, and it is safe to say that it is going to stick around for a very long time indeed. Though the techniques that are used and the ultimate goal of contract killing may differ from era to era, people that have a penchant for killing are always going to be highly in demand.

It is interesting to note how contract killers have evolved. From their origins as assassins to their present day status, contract killers have influenced the world around us in an enormous way and are largely responsible for the way our society works at present. Economic inequality is always going to be an issue, which means that organized crime is always going to exist. And if organized crime will always exist, the same can be said for contract killers and their ilk.

AUDIOBOOKS at RJ Parker Publishing
http://rjparkerpublishing.com/audiobooks.html

Our collection of **CRIMES CANADA** books on Amazon.
http://www.crimescanada.com/

TRUE CRIME Books by RJ Parker Publishing on Amazon.
http://rjpp.ca/ASTORE-TRUECRIME

ACTION / FICTION Books by Bernard DeLeo on Amazon.
http://bit.ly/ACTION-FICTION

RJ Parker Publishing

Follow on *BOOKBUB*

About the Author

RJ Parker, PhD, is an award-winning and bestselling true crime author and owner of RJ Parker Publishing, Inc. He has written over 25 true crime books which are available in eBook, paperback and audiobook editions, and have sold in over 100 countries. He holds certifications in Serial Crime, Criminal Profiling and a PhD in Criminology.

To date, RJ has donated over 3,000 autographed books to allied troops serving overseas and to our wounded warriors recovering in Naval and Army hospitals all over the world. He also donates to Victims of Violent Crimes Canada.

If you are a police officer, firefighter, paramedic or serve in the military, active or retired, RJ gives his eBooks freely in appreciation for your service.

Contact Information

Bookbub:
rjpp.ca/BOOKBUB-RJPARKER
Author's Email:
AuthorRJParker@gmail.com
Publisher's Email:
Agent@RJParkerPublishing.com
Website:
http://m.RJPARKERPUBLISHING.com/
Twitter:
http://www.Twitter.com/realRJParker
Facebook:
https://www.facebook.com/RJParkerPublishing
Amazon Author's Page:
rjpp.ca/RJ-PARKER-BOOKS

** SIGN UP FOR OUR MONTHLY NEWSLETTER **
http://rjpp.ca/RJ-PARKER-NEWSLETTER

The Basement

On March 24, 1987, the Philadelphia Police Department received a phone call from a woman who stated that she had been held captive for the last four months. When police officers arrived at the pay phone from which the call was made, Josefina Rivera told them that she and three other women had been held captive in a basement by a man named Gary Heidnik.  This is a shocking story of kidnapping, rape, torture, mutilation, dismemberment, decapitation, and murder.

The subject matter in this book is graphic

http://rjpp.ca/THE-BASEMENT

Available in eBook, Paperback and Audiobook editions

Serial Killers Encyclopedia

The ultimate reference for anyone compelled by the pathology and twisted minds behind the most disturbing of homicidal monsters. From A to Z, and from around the world, these serial killers have killed in excess of 3,000 innocent victims, affecting thousands of friends and family members. There are monsters in this book that you may not have heard of, but you won't forget them after reading their case. This reference book will make a great collection for true crime aficionados.

WARNING: There are 15 dramatic crime scene photos in this book that some may find extremely disturbing.

http://bit.ly/SK-ENCYCLOPEDIA

Available in eBook, Paperback and Audiobook editions

Parents Who Killed Their Children

What could possibly incite parents to kill their own children?

This collection of "Filicidal Killers" provides a gripping overview of how things can go horribly wrong in once-loving families. Parents Who Killed Their Children depicts ten of the most notorious and horrific cases of homicidal parental units out of control. People like Andrea Yates, Diane Downs, Susan Smith, and Jeffrey MacDonald who received a great deal of media attention. The author explores the reasons; from addiction to postpartum psychosis, insanity to altruism.

Each story is detailed with background information on the parents, the murder scenes, trials, sentencing and aftermath.

http://bit.ly/PARENTSWHOKILLED

Available in eBook, Paperback and Audiobook editions

Appreciation

Thank you to my editor, proofreaders, and cover artist for your support:

~ RJ

Dr. Scott Bonn, Aeternum Designs (book cover), Bettye McKee (editor), Laura Martin, Darlene Horn, Katherine McCarthy, Robyn MacEachern, Caroline Luther, Sandra Miller and Gail Chen

References

1. https://www.fbi.gov/news/stories/murder-for-hire/murder-for-hire
2. http://www.ranker.com/list/famous-hitmen-contract-killers/ranker-crime
3. https://www.psychologytoday.com/blog/wicked-deeds/201404/why-professional-assassins-are-not-serial-killers
4. http://bookinfos.org/the-most-famous-contract-killers-reb.html
5. https://www.theguardian.com/uk-news/2014/jan/25/hitmen-for-hire-secrets-contract-killers
6. https://www.biography.com/people/richard-the-iceman-kuklinski-21360091

RJ Parker

www.ingramcontent.com/pod-product-compliance
Lightning Source LLC
LaVergne TN
LVHW051116080426
835510LV00018B/2077